Howe

# Tales of Teaching

## Or Where Is That School?

Betty Kennedy Tufts

authorHOUSE®

*AuthorHouse™*
*1663 Liberty Drive, Suite 200*
*Bloomington, IN 47403*
*www.authorhouse.com*
*Phone: 1-800-839-8640*

*First published by AuthorHouse 2/12/2009*

*ISBN: 978-1-4389-1249-3 (sc)*

*Printed in the United States of America*
*Bloomington, Indiana*

*This book is printed on acid-free paper.*

## Dedication...


This is for my daughters
Candace
Julie
Mitzi

With love.......

My special thanks go to my friend,
Judy Roy,
who put this all together
and praised me all the way!

# Prologue...

I never had a big dream to become a teacher; to capture young minds and send them out into the world in a blaze of glory. I only knew that I wanted to go to college to learn how to do <u>something</u>. Besides that, those summers off looked pretty good to me as well as a long vacation at Christmas. So teaching it would be.

It didn't take me very long to realize how important these kids in my classes would become to me. They were on my mind even when school was over. Who knew where my teaching would take them? A word of praise or understanding might make all the difference. Even now, after all these years I recall names and faces of so many.

And especially, I believed that <u>education is learning how to live</u> --- and I still do._

## Notes:

Some names have been changed in a few of the tales

About the recipes --- they are a collection from the towns and schools where I taught.

# Contents

# And This Is Where I Went...
# 1940 ---1943

# One

# This Was Gorham...

Let me tell you about the college. First it was called Gorham Normal School, then Gorham State Teachers College and now it is the University of Southern Maine. All the college buildings were on a sizable hill all its own. It was committed totally to training teachers for all of the lucky kids in the State of Maine. And this is where I went in the fall of 1940 --- pumped up with many enthusiastic hopes for teaching success. I was loaded with all my plaid skirts and matching sweaters, tons of my mother's wonderful food (like raspberry turnovers and chocolate cake with fudge frosting,) other goodies from aunts, a few dollars in my pocket from all my relatives who wished me well --- and full of excitement to find my dormitory room and to meet my new roommate, Annette.

A few words about her. She was 4'11" tall, cute as could be and full of moxie. The first day we labeled her "Peanut" and it has stuck to this day --- well, it was a few weeks ago, when our old college crowd got together at Damariscotta Lake. "Peanut" could lighten up the whole place and the two of us made a great team: the "Fantasia Twins." The very first week in our room, Room 28 in Robie Hall, Peanut and I woke up in the night hearing squeaks and scurrying feet running around our room. Roomie crashed out of bed and howled, "What the hell is going on here?" She grabbed a ruler --- metal edges --- and cornered a large size mouse under the radiator. As he struggled to get away, Roomie smacked down hard on the mouse, cutting off half his tail with the brass edged ruler. Then he ran away flat out. We never saw "Shorty" again.

We heard, "When you are out in the field_ _" all the time. They did not mean a field of goldenrod; they meant running a class room full of kids. For that, they mapped out a plan full of required courses, and because of this there was little time left for electives. Otherwise they would not have had a single soul taking "History of Education" for nine solid weeks. They could have told us in 10 minutes flat that Horace Mann was the Father of Public School Education in America and let it go at that. Since I took that course in 1941 no one in this life has asked me who the Father of Education was. Never. That course was tops in useless information.

The same way with Library Science and the Dewey Decimal system when I learned number 395 is for "Etiquette" by Emily Post. That has been a very important part of my life ever since. If I ever put on a formal dinner at my house for the Prime Minister of Canada, I will know how to pull off the seating arrangements, me and Emily Post. It hasn't happened yet, but you never know.

At Gorham in the dorms, there were RULES for everything and bells to remind us. We had a bell to wake us up, a bell for beginning Study Hour at 7:30 and a bell for ending study hour at 10 PM, for lights outs at 10:15. It hardly left us time to clean our teeth before we went to bed. Nobody said it would be like a Rotary Club Picnic.

# Annette's Super Mac and Cheese...

Cook 1 cup macaroni
Mix:
10 oz. sharp cheddar ---melted
2 eggs beaten
1 ½ cup milk

Pour everything into a buttered casserole
Sprinkle crushed Ritz crackers and butter over
macaroni and bake at 350 degrees
*Annette always brings this when our gang gets
together*

## Advanced Reading...

There I was at Teacher's College in Gorham, Maine and this is when the rubber hits the road. It was September 1940 when we 18 year olds showed up on the campus in our smart new blazers and page boy haircuts, full of pep and ready to train as teachers.

Reality set in when all of us in D2, meaning that section of the freshman class, not my academic standing, (thanks be to God for that) went to our very first class: <u>Advanced Reading</u> with Mr. Smart. Mr. Smart looked like a model for "Old Spice" Cologne and Shaving Cream. Old Spice was the cool men's cologne that year. Mr. Smart was young and handsome, well turned out, but dull, fired up with a bunch of theories about education. He was very serious about the thing. He didn't laugh much; he was really all business: teaching us <u>Advanced Reading</u>. This was all a conundrum to me. What did <u>Advanced Reading</u> mean? Advanced for the kids we would be teaching? Or did it mean advanced reading for us? How could we learn anything about advanced reading when we didn't even know about <u>primary</u> reading? Of course, we had heard about Dick and Jane and Spot a few times and I thought that was where any reading started. Maybe Advanced Reading was serious reading with no pictures to help out. That class two days a week left me glassy-eyed, trying to work things out. I thought that if this is how teacher training would be, I would never last here. And then I discovered a wonderful remedy for boredom in class. I could sit there in my assigned seat and pretend I was taking notes when I was really making up crossword puzzles. I made up some really good ones too. My puzzles were as good as any the <u>Sunday New York Times</u> came up with.

After that, things slowed down a bit when other classes made more sense until we met up with <u>Advanced Arithmetic</u> where the instructor introduced us to the "Casting Out Nines." Did you ever hear of it? Why would we cast out nines? What did we have against <u>nines</u>? It ranked right up there with Advanced Reading. It seemed to me that whoever set up these classes was making a serious mistake here. They had this big thing about <u>advanced</u>. Didn't they know we should have primary stuff first? As for me, I kept right on making up crossword puzzles which was a lot more inspiring and had just as much future for me as casting out nines.

# Butter Horns...

Beat together:
1 cup butter softened
1 – 12 ounce carton cottage cheese
Then add:
2 cups flour
Dash of salt

Blend until smooth
Cover and refrigerate four hours or overnight
Divide into 3 parts; form into balls
Roll out flat into circles 12" in diameter
Roll each wedge from wide to small end
Place on greased cookie sheet with tips turned under
Bake 350 degrees for 30 minutes

These can be frosted with light confectioner's sugar, milk and vanilla

# Dorm Life...

I thought dormitory life was great. There was always someone around to carry on with, and always something going on. When times got a little dull, someone was sure to come up with a sensational plan to liven things up.

In our dorm it was customary to share "food from home," Come one come all. Yet there was a pouty freshman on our floor who ignored that plan. Her father owned a sardine packing plant on the coast and when she got back from a weekend at home she was always loaded down with cans of sardines, enough for Admiral Byrd's expedition to the Arctic. We got fed up with her when she borrowed our can opener time and time again and never offered us a single sardine. She was as fat as a plumped up feather bed and she didn't need all those glossy sardines. It would have been nicer and easier if we had just given her a new can opener of her own but that would have spoiled all the fun. One night after she borrowed our can opener one more time and we didn't get a whiff of those tasty fish, someone came up with a great idea of getting even. The plan was to take out the pins in the hinges on her door in the dorm, before she came up from dinner. It was like an explosion on the Russian front when she opened her door and it fell flat, crashing to the floor. When she left to look for the pins, someone brought those back and swiped the door. Looking back all these years, I wonder whether we were immature or just plain mean. We still never got a sardine. I don't think she ever figured out the reason for the door caper.

We ate our meals together in East Hall Dining Room, including some of the men from their boarding houses down town. It was like eating in a restaurant but with a set of rules. We were expected to come to the dining hall in correct attire (no curlers, pin curls or bathrobes) and on Sunday we were expected to dress for dinner. That meant dresses or suits and no Mickey Mouse sweatshirts. Actually I thought that was just fine – all of us looking our best and I guess that idea has stayed with me all these years. Sometimes "looking good" is half the battle –– any battle.

# Angel Biscuits...

Dissolve:
1 pkg. dry yeast
¼ cup warm water

Mix together:
2 ½ cups flour
½ tsp. baking soda
½ tsp. salt
1/8 cup sugar

Cut in ½ cup shortening
Stir in 1 cup butter milk, then yeast and water mixture

Blend thoroughly and refrigerate in covered bowl or make into biscuits

Roll out and cut with biscuit cutter --- place in greased pan

Let biscuits rise slightly

Pop into oven at 400 degrees until brown

## The Yellow Arrow to Portland...

In the middle of the campus was Corthell Hall where most of the classes were held, but how many people knew there was a huge yellow arrow painted on the roof top directing air traffic TO PORTLAND? I came across that great discovery one Saturday afternoon after 2 friends, boys, gave up trying to teach me how to play pool. By then they knew my limitations with any ball; baseball, softball, tennis ball, ping pong ball, --- you name it. I was beginning to be paranoid about it after a date to the movies with a popular guy who spent most of the evening telling me how well coordinated another girl, Gerry, was, on and on. I did not like that much since I was not on good terms with coordination. I could sing well, I got good grades and I had a lot of friends, but no one would ever compliment me on my coordination playing ball. When I got back to my room that night I sputtered to my roommate that if he thought Gerry was so well coordinated he could take her to the movies next time, not me.

Back to the roof --- one of the three of us on the roof was a cute freshman everyone was crazy over. He broke into song and dance on that roof singing "Give My Regards to Broadway." He just cracked me up. He was so good. And after that whenever I looked up at Corthell Hall I could see Dickie Nelson doing a great job of tap dancing all around that yellow arrow; TO PORTLAND.

# Sweet Cinnamon Biscuits...

Combine and stir well:
2 cups flour
1 tbs. baking powder
1 tsp. salt
¼ tsp. baking soda

Add and stir well:
¼ cup vegetable oil
¾ cup butter milk

Knead the dough on a lightly floured surface until smooth

Roll dough into a 15" x *8' rectangle
Preheat oven to 400 degrees
Grease a 9" round baking pan
Spread 1 stick softened butter over the dough

Mix together:
¾ cup sugar
1 tsp. cinnamon

Roll up rectangle in jelly roll fashion, starting from one long side
Pinch seam to seal
Cut the roll into 1 ½" slices
Arrange the slices, cut side up in prepared pan
Bake 15 to 20 minutes

## Archery, Anyone?...

I was really excited about Physical Education since it was a new experience for me. Our little high school in my home town did not offer it. The only Phys. Ed we got was walking home for lunch. The instructor of Physical Education here was Miss Foster, athletic in form and full of pep and vinegar. I could tell by her looks on my first day in her class that she would wear us all out with her physical training ideas. You know the type. I went all out for this class and bought the whole gym outfit; ugly navy blue bloomers (which were definitely out of style for even then.) Those bloomers hung in a discouraged way down to my knees, with a white blouse and a dark blue woolen vest which was hotter than Hitty (whoever that was) in those warm fall days. We looked like Christopher Columbus when he landed on the beach in those baggy panty hose. It itched as well, but I was determined to look the part of an All – American Sport. Actually, the most important part of our outfits were the white sneakers, all alike. We were told to print our names in bold black letters across the fronts of the sneakers; upside down to us but just right for Miss Foster to read when she lined us up to take attendance. That opened up a whole new aspect of switching sneakers for identification, wondering whether she could recognize our faces, or our sneakers.

Along with class time we had another requirement for the course. Each one of us had to play in one sport which could be field hockey, basketball, soft ball or archery. One thing I could do without was chasing a ball --- any ball, up and down the field and getting my shins kicked with a hockey stick. The same thing with soft ball: it didn't appeal to me to be running bases in hot weather. I didn't want anything to do with a <u>ball.</u> I didn't want to throw it, kick it, hit it, chase it or catch it. I didn't want to suit up in a moth eaten uniform with baggy legs (the uniforms not mine) and I surely didn't want to be on a team that didn't want me---they all knew by then that I was no shining athletic star. So I chose <u>archery</u> for my sport. It seemed noble to me to stand with perfect posture and a sharp eye and let that arrow zing into the target. Not only that I didn't have to run anywhere. I could just stand there without sweating and let the arrows go northeast or southwest. It didn't make any difference to me. Then I came up with a plan. I could shoot those arrows into that oil cloth-covered bale of hay and afterward I could draw a bull's eye around each hole where my arrow had landed. I really impressed a lot of people and it made me look good. I got so I liked the sport but I was never as good as William Tell when he shot the apple off his son's head that time.

One day Miss Foster introduced us to Interpretive Dance. That's when you tell a story by dancing and active imaginary gestures. Her specialty was Jack and the Beanstock, the entire story told in dance, weird as all get out to me since our little town had never especially gone in for this kind of art. She stretched and reached high in the air on the dreamed up beanstock and cowered briskly from the giant, neither of which were real, but it didn't impress me much. The best part of this was that we didn't have to do laps around the gym that day, which I never thought had any reason or point. Every now and then we begged Miss Foster to do that routine so that we could slouch against the bleachers and watch <u>her</u> get all tired and sweaty instead of us. Let me tell you she was all business and it was tough to keep up with her.

# Connie's Poppy Seed Bread...

Combine:
3 cups flour
2 ½ cups sugar
1 ½ tsp. salt
1 ½ tsp. baking powder

In smaller cowl, mix:
3 beaten eggs
1 ½ cups milk
1 cup & 2 tbs. oil
3 tbs. poppy seeds
1 ½ tsp. vanilla
1 ½ tsp. almond extract
1 ½ tsp. Durkee's butter flavoring

Combine both mixtures and beat all together.

Pour into 2 greased and floured 9"x5" loaf pans.

Bake 325 for 1 hour.

As bread cools, mix:
½ cup orange juice
¾ cup sugar
½ almond extract
½ tsp. oil

Heat topping until sugar melts

Poke small holes in bread loaves and pour topping all over

*I first found this recipe at an antiques show in Portsmouth This is a real treat.*

.

# The Follies of 1942...

Miss Foster gave us a crash course in tap dancing. Fred Astaire and Ginger Rogers were big then in "Forty Second Street" and "Follies of 1942." We didn't give them any competition to speak of but we thought it was a nice change of activity. Then one night we came up with a clever plan for the tap dancing. We had a classmate who studied all the time and got top marks. Since all classes were graded relatively, everyone was scored by the top student's mark. At this time we had coming up, an exam in Adolescent Psychology which would be tough. We knew Kay was up in her room on the third floor studying hard, planning to ace that exam. Someone got the bright idea that if we went up to Kay's room and tap danced all evening, she wouldn't have time to hit that Psych book. Since it was a dorm rule that all lights had to be out at 10:30 PM or you got a pink slip --- 3 of them and you were in trouble with the house committee. I was scared to death of those upper classmen when I was a freshman, but as a junior I was elected to that committee myself. You know that old saying "If you can't fight 'em, join 'em."

Back to tap dancing up in Kay's room on the third floor. We asked her to show us that new tapping routine. We tapped and tapped and tapped, taking turns and getting all worn out. Not only that, we had to supply our own music---we had to <u>hum</u> which wasn't too bad as long as we all hummed the same song. Even the kids in the room beneath Kay's rapped on the pipes to tell us to knock it off. Anyway, when we left, we <u>dragged</u> our twinkle toes that had been dancing for 2 hours. We didn't have any energy left to crack those psychology notes. Well, we took that exam the next day and of course Kay got an A anyway. And what did the Rockettes get? We all got C's but we were really good tap dancers. Miss Foster was impressed.

# Merle's Coffee Cake...

In a large bowl, beat together:
1 pkg. yellow cake mix
1 pkg. dry butterscotch instant pudding mix
4 eggs
¾ cup oil
¾ cup water

## TOPPING

Mix:
½ stick of butter
½ cup sugar
1 tsp. cocoa
1 tsp. cinnamon

Pour batter in a 9" x 13" greased pan

Spoon topping on cake batter

Swirl topping into cake

Bake at 350 degrees until sides loosen from pan

# We Studied Birds...

In 1942 I had completed my first 2 years of teachers' college. I had all those courses to turn me out as a teacher --- ready to save the world. I had studied all kinds of psychology and that was only a beginning. We had history (all kinds), political science, ethics (that was a course to tell us all the rules for decent living) and primary arithmetic which I hated. How long did it take to teach kids how to add? Sometimes I had to wonder why these instructors made such a fuss out of simple things like primary arithmetic ; 2 + 2 always make 4 and 3 + 3 always make 6. There it is; the facts without all the hype.

In our first year we had a course of Bird Study with a very active teacher, Miss Allen, who could scale fences, stonewalls and swamps faster than any of us who were half her age. It all had to do with <u>incentive</u>; she wanted to find all those birds in the wild, when I was contented to see them in the air and let them alone. I knew robins, blue jays, crows and sea gulls (which any kid from the coast of Maine knows.) That was it for me and I was happy enough with that. We got our workouts when Miss Allen led our class on bird walks in Alden's Woods, looking for any bird we could find and listening for any bird we could hear. We trudged along behind Miss Allen when all of a split second she would stop still (when all of us behind her fell back like a bunch of dominos) and she would say in a low tone "Did you hear that? It sounds like a meadow lark to me." I never could hear a thing except my squishy shoes that had gone through the swamp.

It soon became apparent that we were in for a tough tramp. It was no fluff, I can tell you that. My friend Adeline and I were fed up with the whole thing and tired of birds in particular. Birds did not hold much attraction for me at that time in my life. I thought our instructor was being pretty nosey---tracking all those poor birds who just wanted to just hang out and lay eggs. My friend Adeline and I had an idea. When the class went ahead 10 feet she and I dropped back 10 feet, hiding in the bushes until we came out on campus covered with black fly bites and of course those soggy shoes. The rest of the class and Miss Allen never missed us because they were smitten with all those birds.

A big part of Bird Study was making and presenting a BIRD BOOK. When I had showed up on campus as a freshman, the two most important and talked about subjects were:

1. The May Ball
2. The Bird Book

As far as I was concerned, given a little time I could handle The May Ball, but at last is the Bird Book for which we cut and pasted and colored every picture and article about a bird we could ever find. I had my 4 aunts at home collecting every picture of a bird they found. They really got into this project. Even in a doctor's office waiting room or a hair salon they quietly snipped out pictures of every feathered friend they came across. Even <u>Popular Mechanics</u> was not safe because once in a while there would be a pattern for a bird house. Our bird books, I thought, were graded on how many pictures there were and I was determined to have a winner.

I thought it would be a nice touch to include a poem about you-know-what. I hit the library and found this one by Alfred Tennyson who was famous for his classy poems.

*The Eagle*

*He clasps the crag with crooked lands,*

*Close to the sun in lonely lands,*

*Ring'd with the azure world he stands*

*The wrinkled sea beneath him crawls*

*He watches from his mountain walls,*

*And like a thunderbolt he falls.*

*Alfred Tennyson*

The instructor was impressed; my bird book was an A+.

# Quick Peanut Butter Cookies...

Combine:
2 cups sugar
1 tsp. baking soda
2 eggs beaten
2 tsp. vanilla
2 cups really chunky peanut butter (Can be low-fat)

Mix together, shape into balls and then roll in sugar

Place balls on greased cookie sheet

Bake at 350 degrees for 11 to 12 minutes

*This recipe makes 24 large or 30 small cookies.*
*These are the best peanut butter cookies I have ever made.*

## I Found My Major...

Finally I caught up with the best college teacher I could ever have; Miss Esther Wood, who taught all classes of American History. She was a small person and she wore her hair in a brown braid that circled her head in a quaint style like her grandmother in Blue Hill Maine would have done. During my first class with her I knew I was going to like her. To start with, she had a downeast twang in her speech. It was fresh air to me after hearing so many native born State-of-Mainers try to talk in a fake Massachusetts or New York accent, God forbid. I figured if she had degrees from Radcliffe College and could hang on to her Maine way of speaking, so could I.

To begin with, I loved history and political science anyway, and she made even the most mundane facts and events seem interesting. I had at last found my major. It was history all the way! Her spin on the Sherman Anti-Trust Laws, the story of the Mormons and their journey to Utah, or the real scoop on the Indians were all real to me. I took every course she taught and I was determined to teach like she did; walking around the room, using dramatic tones of voice, writing on the black boards and making maps of everything. She made us alert wondering what she would do next. There was no time in her class to make up crossword puzzles. I wanted to make the most of whaling out of Nantucket, and the spectacular travels of the Lewis and Clark Expedition that traveled west to the Pacific. I loved it and a dramatic teacher could make all the difference when teaching history and government. I was going to carry it off like Miss Wood. I worked my head off to keep up with her. I loved the stories of history and people and the times in which they lived. When we were in the middle of the Westward Movement when Americans went west in their Conestoga wagons or prairie schooners, I would have jumped right on one of those wagons and gone along with those pioneers. I would have known the way because hadn't Miss Wood made maps on the board of the Oregon Trail? When we studied the Civil War, she expected us to learn the strategies of the generals on both sides. Miss Wood was the best; she made us think and identify with people of the past. I could do that. I never bothered much with historic dates; the people were much more important to me. I loved teaching these things and how our lives are influenced by the past. And al ways in my classes, I remembered Miss Wood and how she would have taught it.

# Nanaimo Bars...

Put in bowl:
½ cup soft butter
2 tbs. cocoa
½ tsp. vanilla
1 egg

Set bowl into pan of boiling water. Stir until butter has melted

Mix together:
2 cups graham cracker crumbs
1 cup coconut
½ cup chopped walnuts

Add cocoa mixture

Pack into 9" pan

**Icing**
Mix:
4 tbs. butter
2 tbs. milk
2 tbs. vanilla instant pudding mix
2 cups confectioner's sugar

Spread over chocolate mixture and let harden in marble effect with 2 squares semi sweet chocolate and 1 tbs. butter.

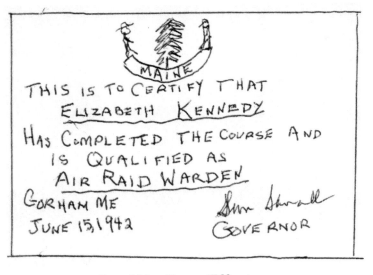

## Our Wartime Effort...

In that fall of 1942 the war was foremost in all our lives and we tried to think of something we could do for the war effort besides blacking out our windows and eating cottage cheese on our toast instead of butter. (We wondered where all that butter was going. Did the army get butter on their toast?)

Then the Poetry Club thought it would be a great stroke of kindness to collect books for the Army base in Portland. We liked that idea and set the date on a Saturday to canvass the town, knocking on doors and asking for books. My friend Adeline and I got a child's cart and spent that day hauling those books around one street and down the next until the cart was loaded and very heavy. We had a plan. Before we turned in those books, Adeline and I sat up that Saturday night writing our names and phone numbers in every book, even the JKL part of the Britannica Encyclopedia, the only one of the series we got. We knew our plan was a good one. We could just imagine a lonely soldier in Fort Williams calling us for a telephone conversation. Yes, it was a good idea, but that's all it was. We never got a call. Maybe those soldiers just were not interested in reading those books. They didn't know what they were missing.

Then we heard about a course for Air Raid Wardens. About six of our crowd tripped down to the local high school every Tuesday night where we had instruction in handling air raid disasters. We had a First Aid course and then we went on to the identification of foreign air craft over our part of Maine. I have kept that little card of certification of me, a State of Maine Air Raid Warden ever since. Every time I look up my driver's license in my wallet I come across that little card of 1942.

Back to the air raid warden's course. As part of the program, Dr. Bailey---president of the college---thought it would be wise to have air raid drills in the dormitories and he made sure we used our newly acquired skills to carry these out. It meant we had to clear all people from all floors of the dorms. That was O.K. by me until I realized the

4<sup>th</sup> floor was spooky and empty, especially in the dark. If I ever met anyone up there I would have fallen over dead in my 19 year old tracks. Then all my gumption kicked in. I charged up those stairs like Teddy Roosevelt led his Rough Riders up San Juan Hill in Cuba in the Spanish American War. It was not fun but I did my best.

## I had Talent...

One more story about Gorham. It was during graduation week when everyone was signing names and comments in yearbooks that had just come out. I was with a group of guys and girls, including Virginia Hood, a beautiful girl who was a very talented musician. She played piano as a professional and we all admired her. During our book signing, her yearbook and mine got switched around and someone, thinking he was writing in Virginia's book, wrote "To the most talented girl in Gorham" in <u>my</u> book. I didn't mention it to anyone because I thought it looked pretty good for me. When summer vacation came and I took my yearbook home, my mother read it all. (That was in the days when yearbooks were decent enough for your mother to read.) Finally Mom saw that praise "To the most talented girl in Gorham" and of course she thought the writer meant <u>me</u> and she said, so pleased and proudly, "They think a lot of you in Gorham, don't they, Betty?" And I replied "Yes they do, Mom." Why spoil my mother's impression?

# Janice's Marvel Pie...

Melt and blend together over hot water:
1 pkg. semisweet chocolate bits
3 tbs. milk
2 tbs. sugar

Cool

Add:
4 egg yokes, one at a time, beating after each addition
1 tsp. vanilla
Beat until stiff:
4 egg whites

Fold into chocolate mixture

Pour into cooled 9" baked pie shell.

Chill and garnish with whipped cream

# Livermore – 1942…

# TWO

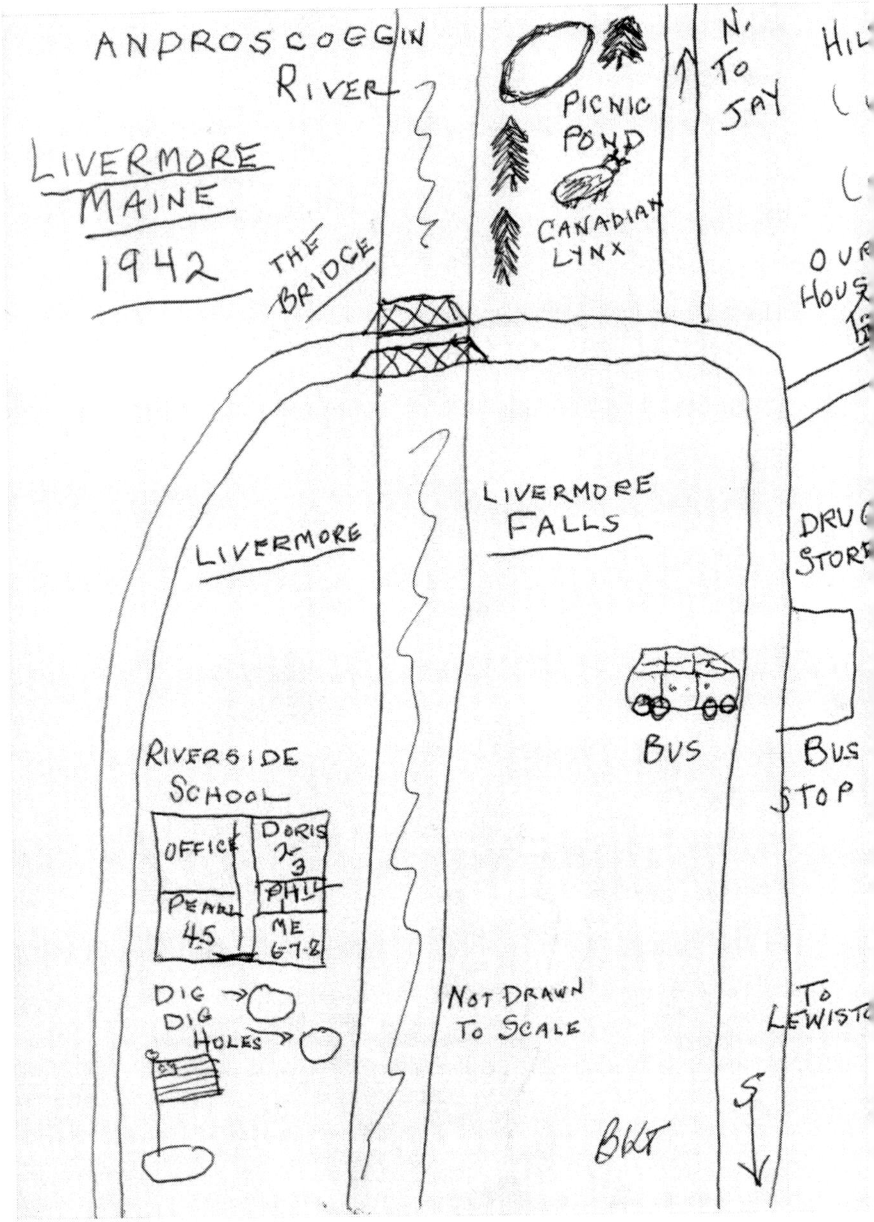
ANDROSCOGGIN RIVER
LIVERMORE MAINE
1942
THE BRIDGE
PICNIC POND
CANADIAN LYNX
N. TO JAY
OUR HOUSE
LIVERMORE FALLS
LIVERMORE
DRUG STORE
BUS
BUS STOP
RIVERSIDE SCHOOL
OFFICE
DORIS 2 3
PHIL
PEARL 4 5
ME 6 7 8
DIG DIG HOLES
NOT DRAWN TO SCALE
TO LEWISTO
S
BKT

# Big Change in Plans...

In the summer of 1942 I was looking forward to that September when I would finally do some real classroom teaching. I had been assigned to the 8th grade in the Training School on campus with a critic teacher who had the reputation of one of the best. I was anxious to see whether I even <u>liked</u> teaching; and it was about time I found out.

So ---- imagine my surprise and confusion when 2 weeks before Labor Day I got a letter from Doctor Bailey, president of the college. He had a wild plan for me and 3 of my classmates. Doctor Bailey said we had been chosen to take over and run an elementary school in northern Maine. Was he nuts? None of us had ever faced a school room full of kids before! He explained that due to a lack of teachers in Maine (as well as in most every state in wartime 1942,) the college had agreed to this ambitious project. One bright spot in this crazy scheme was the fact that all 4 of us were close friends and we could count on each other for support --- and even <u>fun</u> if we could find any. Phyllis would take grade 1, Doris would have grades 2 & 3, Pearl would have grades 4 & 5 and I got grades 6, 7, and 8; about 20 kids for each of us. Over all we would have a critic teacher in the school to offer help and direction, mark our progress and grade us accordingly.

The whole thing was a tremendous undertaking for the 4 of us and a great responsibility for the college as well. They were counting on us.

The college found us an apartment and that was it; they backed off and we were on our own --- like throwing the Christians into a pit of hungry lions. Same thing.

# Julie's Lemon Crème Bars...

Combine and set aside:
1 can condensed milk
½ cup lemon juice

Combine:
1 ½ cups flour
1 cup quick oatmeal
1 cup firmly packed brown sugar

Mix until crumbly

Press half the crumb mixture into a greased 13 x 9 pan

Spread with lemon mixture

Crumble remaining mixture over all

Bake 350 degrees

Bars will be soft

Chill, then cut into bars.

## Just Where Is That School?...

After we got to this town, Livermore, the Sunday before Labor Day to take over that school, our first move of course was to find it! There was no school person anywhere around, nor any interested parent on hand to welcome us or even to look us over. An ego trip it was not. All we knew was that the school was across the Androscoggin River, and that included half of Androscoggin County. There we were wandering all over the place without a clue. "Across the Androscoggin" did not narrow it down too much. Finally someone in the drug store told us to go across the bridge and turn south. At least now we were headed in the right direction and on foot of course, because none of us had a car. We were searching for that school like Richard the Lion

Hearted hunted for the Holy Grail. We almost missed the school because it was down on the side of a hill. There it was; a pathetic building that looked like an abandoned chicken coop that no self respecting hen would call home. Sometime in the past, part of the building had been covered with brick-looking shingles. There was not one redeeming thing about the outside of that school to inspire us. We tried doors and windows to get in; and right there we were ready to ditch this whole ridiculous operation. We must have presented an interesting sight to the natives when they saw us boosting each other up to find a loose window to crawl through, with one of us holding back the branches of an old pine tree so that we could get up on the window sill; all 4 of us college girls in our snappy monogrammed sweaters and our brand new saddle shoes. (I always got a new pair of saddles every fall; one year brown and white and the next year black & white. One year I found a pair of dark brown suede, actually 1 ½ sizes too big for me, but they were gorgeous even if I had to wear a pair of heavy socks to keep them from flapping at the heels.)

Back to us propping each other up to the windows. Once in a while a car passing by stopped and backed up to get a better look at all this. Then a former janitor at the school happened to drive by and wondered what this performance was all about. He solved our problem when he came up with the key. We were in!

We sorted out each of the rooms by the size of the desks and chairs. Then in my classroom I found the greatest treasure of all on a shelf beside a half eaten jar of rancid peanut butter: a copy of the <u>Maine State School Curriculum</u>. It told us what should be taught in each grade. Wow! It was a <u>eureka </u>moment. We matched the course of study in each grade to the textbooks we found hanging around in each room. Piece of cake! We were so lucky now to have some direction. How else would we know when to teach long division or parts of speech to these kids in Androscoggin County  Maine who were just dying to learn about them?

At last we thought we could be ready for the <u>First Day</u> which was tomorrow!

# Apricot Bars...

Cream:
½ lb. butter
1 cup sugar

Mix until fluffy

Add:
2 egg yolks beaten
2 cups flour
1 cup chopped nuts

Spoon half the mixture into a greased 9" square cake pan

Spread evenly

Then spread ¾ cup apricot preserves on top of nut mixture.

Top all of it with rest of nut mixture

Bake at 325 degrees for 1 hour or until top is golden brown

# The First Day...

On Tuesday, THE FIRST DAY, we tripped along over the river --- by now you know it is the Androscoggin --- and down the road to the school. We were all dolled up and bright eyed, hair just so after a night of sleeping on curlers and pin curls, wearing bright red lipstick and scarlet nail polish. This was our first day of teaching school and we were giving it our best shot.

We stood in the doorways of our classrooms, smiling warmly when all these kids looked us over. We depended on the kids to know where they were supposed to go. And then at the same time as the kids started to arrive, <u>Miss Perkins</u> showed up for the first time. She was our critic teacher who was there to advise us and help us along the way with advice on how to teach. Well, that's what she was there for. It never happened.

During the next months she was the Rottweiler in our lives. She barked out orders, snapped us to attention and sniffed out all our plans. We should have realized it to begin with when we saw her cold steel blue eyes. From then on, we were scared to death of her. I still used the <u>Maine State Curriculum for Public Schools</u> to find my way, but that was not good enough for her. She criticized every move we made, all in front of our classes of kids, so often that our students began giving us sympathetic looks whenever that doorknob turned and she came in at full steam. She was a person who would complain if you hanged her with a new rope.

Back to the first day. After I wrote my name on the blackboard we saluted the flag and said the Lord's Prayer. Then whatever came next was up to me. All I had was a list of the kids' names and the grades where they belonged, so I had each one of them stand and say his name. Then what? All those kids --- 20 of them in my 3 grades --- were staring at me and waiting for me to tell them what to do next. I didn't even know myself but I figured passing out books would be a good start. I passed out those books with great flair, acting like I knew what I was doing. I didn't have to worry --- all the kids knew the ropes and I knew right away I could count on them.

# Priscilla's Toffee Treats...

Beat:
1 cup butter
1 cup firmly packed brown sugar
1 beaten egg yolk
1 tsp. vanilla

Combine and add to butter:
2 cups flour
¼ tsp. salt

Mix well.

Spread batter into lightly greased 13" x 9" x 2" pan

Bake at 350 degrees for 25-30 minutes

Crust will be soft

Remove from oven and immediately arrange 5 – 1.65 ounce milk chocolate bars on top of hot crust.

Let stand until chocolate softens

Spread evenly over crust

Sprinkle with chopped pecans

Let cool in pans

# The Kids in Riverside School...

All our pupils in that school were pretty average kids except for a bad egg here and there. Pearl had one of those in the 5th grade who called her a "big baboon," after which Pearl dragged him into Miss Perkins' office. Miss Perkins took the boy by the ear back to Pearl's classroom and made him get down on his knees and apologize. (Hmmmm---------what Miss Perkins didn't know was that we called her "Miss Dumbo.")

Phyllis had a boy in first grade who never spoke a word for the first 2 weeks of school. He had beautiful dark eyes which were studying everything in the room, but he never made a peep. Phyllis thought he was mute – or maybe not the brightest kid on the planet. When Phyllis realized he had a big brother in the 7th grade, she asked the brother "Was he mute? Was he deaf?"

Maurice said, "He can't speak English, only French." Well, wasn't Phyllis just lucky to find out that kid was not disabled, but just couldn't speak English? Phyllis worked very hard with that boy. She got him so that he could actually make simple sentences in English and tell all the objects in the room. I wondered how his parents felt about that since they had never bothered to teach him English at home.

All I remember about Phyllis' first grade was all those kids lying down, stretched out on the hallway floor with their feet wagging in the air expecting Phyllis to put on their boots. Most of those boots and rubbers were way too small anyway. They were hand-me-downs, and sizes didn't matter in a big family. My 3 upper grades seemed easier after I saw all the first grade feet wagging in the air like bull rushes in the wind.

There were some outstanding kids in the upper grades that I had. There was Dwight Lamb who had bright red hair. He was a charmer, bright as all get out. One day in the fall when it was warm for October, Dwight said "Miss Kennedy, if you don't open that window, you are going to have roast Lamb over here. Then there was Norman in the 8th grade, a wonderful boy who stood out in the crowd, an all around good kid. His 2 best friends were "Happy" and Ernest. The three of them made my life a lot easier in the classroom.

# Christmas Tree Cookies...

Cream:
½ cup butter

Add:
1 cup sugar
1 egg
2 cups flour
1 tsp. baking powder
¼ tsp. salt

Chill

Roll out to 1/8" thickness

Cut in all kinds of shapes

Bake at 325 degrees for 8 minutes

When cool, decorate tops

These can be Christmas cookies, or Halloween cookies or any other shape.

I found these in a <u>Woman's </u>Day magazine 50 years ago
and  they are still the very best.

# Music, Art and Phys Ed…

It was no surprise to us that this school did not provide programs for the extras like art, music and physical education. It was up to us to do our own thing in our classrooms. We could do that ---and we did.

I loved to sing, so it was fun to teach my 3 grades a lot of old tunes like "Swanée River," "Billy Boy" and "You Are My Sunshine." Their favorite was "When It's Round-up Time in Texas." It goes something like "When the bloom is one the sage," but they loved the chorus, "….drinking coffee from a can." They belted that out in great shape, like they were ready to grab a horse and head for the Rio Grande.

The closest we came to instrumental music was humming through tissue paper folded on a comb. Actually it was toilet paper that carried the tune the best because it was thin, being the cheapest

T.P. that this school could buy (no frills in this school.) The kids really got into this. Grades 6 & 7 sang the words, and for the responsibility of this classy act I let the 8th graders cut loose on the paper and combs. They were pretty good at that, especially on the high notes, except sometimes they blew right through that cheap paper. Then it was a cappela all the way.

All the kids liked art class; maybe not because they had any great talent, but because they loved the freedom and the unstructured classes that were necessary because they had to take turns with the scissors, paint, crayons and glue. Actually, the classroom usually turned into a free-for-all every Friday afternoon with all that sharing and someone always getting smeared with glue or doused with water colors. That's why I always scheduled art on Friday afternoon so that when school was over after the art class they could go home, and I didn't have to quiet them down. They could use up all their exuberance on the school bus on the way home.

I had to come up with art projects that all 3 grades in my room could do. Can you imagine how I could keep up with 25 kids doing 3 different projects? I bought paper plates for our project. I showed them how to color them or paint them with water colors (big mistake) then glue together, one plate to a half plate making a pocket. They put a piece of yarn in a hole at the top to hang it. Now what in the world they would ever do with these gems was beyond me, but the kids all thought they were nifty. This just shows how a little art can go a long way.

We were not too concerned about Physical Education in that school because most of our kids walked to school every day and a lot of them worked on their farms at home. So we used fun and games for our Phys Ed. We played airplane, hopscotch and statue tag. The four of us teachers took turns for outside duty seeing that the kids were safe and all getting fresh air.

Pearl was really very good at playground duty. She organized games, choosing sides and having races. Not me. All the kids ever did when I was out there was dig, dig, dig in the playground. They used pieces of old boards that they came up with from who knows where. They would dig and dig one big hole for 3-4 days until the hole was 4 feet across and I foot deep. Then one day, with no words spoken, they would fill it in and start digging a new hole somewhere else. This was lost on me. None of the psychology courses I ever had covered the reasons for this behavior and the kids all seemed to like it, so I let them keep on digging.

Who knows when some of them might join the Foreign Legion --- and knowing how to dig a hole in the sand might come in handy.

# Shirley's Date Balls...

Melt in fry pan:
½ cup butter
¾ cup sugar
1 cup chopped dates

Add:
1 tbs. milk
1 beaten egg

Stir over low heat for 15 minutes

While still warm add:
3 cups Rice Krispies
¾ cup walnuts

Shape into balls and roll in sugar

Makes 50 – 52 balls

# Calling Out the Troops...

Our critic teacher, Miss Perkins continued to harass us. It was not unusual for her to blow into our classrooms and in the guttural tones of a platoon sergeant, ask us what we were teaching. Often she would trash our lessons that we had spent much time on. On the other hand, she was top dog here and we worried what grades she would give us on our teaching; those grades that would be so important on our transcripts. I did have one secret satisfaction though. When she wrote on the black board, her upper arms flapped like the Stars and Stripes in a gale of wind. Miss America, she wasn't.

Since we had had no word at all from the college, I decided that the college would hear from us. I spent one entire weekend composing a definitive letter to Dr. Bailey and Miss Hastings, the Director of Student Teaching. It was a very forceful this-is-how-it-is letter. I told them how hard we had been working, finding our own way with no help from Miss Perkins. I told them how miserable she had been.

It felt wonderful to me to be writing it all down! Well, my 3 buddies, Doris, Pearl and Phyllis, were horrified that I would even think of sending a letter like that to the <u>president</u> of the college and to Miss Hastings. My friends said they wouldn't let me do it; but first they had to find it. I tucked it under the sink, beside the Bab-o can (which was a good place to put it since we never used Bab-o.)

Well --- on Monday morning I mailed the letter and before the week was out, Dr. Bailey and Miss Hastings arrived at our school in Dr. Bailey's dark red Packard. They brought us goodies from the college dining room and did everything but pat our heads. They talked to us together and they talked to us separately and they spent time in Miss Perkins' office with the door closed. They told us that every thing would be better. It wasn't --- and we knew we would have to handle the situation ourselves. Miss P. stayed in her office all day, only now and then walking into our classrooms and causing some kind of trouble.

We looked forward to weekends when we could keep away from her. That didn't work either. One weekend when Doris and I went to Boston for a weekend (I with Stan and Doris with a blind date,) wouldn't you just know she was right there on the same bus as we were --- coming and going --- and not missing a thing.

# Praline Crispies...

Arrange on a foil lined baking sheet:
15 double or 30 single graham crackers

Place 2 sticks butter in a pan and bring to a boil

Add 1 cup brown sugar

Return to boil and boil 2 minutes

Immediately pour over the graham crackers

Sprinkle with 1 cup chopped pecans or walnuts

Bake at 350 degrees for 10 minutes

Let stand for 10 minutes

Cool thoroughly

Slide off baking sheet and cut into squares

Makes lots!

## Chocolate Saves My Career...

Finally, one Friday when the situation at school with Miss Perkins had only gotten wicked desperate, I was fed up with this dumb movie I seemed to be in. I was following the <u>Maine State School Curriculum</u> because it seemed to be the logical and correct rules to follow. But we should have been given some direction in how to teach, how to handle problem kids (good thing we didn't have many), or how to deal with teaching more than one class at a time. All day long I feared she would barge into my classroom and ruin everything. And, don't forget, she was giving me my grades. I knew I was doing well, but who knows what she was doing to my records?

Then on that Friday, when I was completely wiped out and feeling like Custer making his last stand, I packed up all my clothes and hair curlers and laundry soap and headed down over the hill to the bus stop at the drug store. My partners all helped me juggle my stuff into the drug store/bus stop. I didn't know where I was going only that I was leaving Miss Perkins forever. Then Pearl, ever the optimist, figured I would feel better with a hot fudge sundae. With chocolate fudge all around, my bus came and went. I never could leave a fudge sundae half eaten so I sat right there. It was just what Pearl had planned, and then we all struggled back up the hill with my stuff. I settled in for more of Miss Perkins. At the end, my career was saved.

# Jean's Pudding Cookies...

Cream:
1 cup softened butter
1 cup vegetable oil
1 cup sugar
1 cup confectioner's sugar

Add:
2 eggs
1 tsp. vanilla
1 pkg. instant lemon pudding (or other flavor)

Combine:
4 cups flour
1 tsp. cream of tartar
1 tsp. baking soda

Gradually add to the creamed mix.

Drop by spoonfuls on greased cookie sheet.

Bake in a 350 degree oven for 12 to 15 mins.

Yield 7-8 dozen

# Canadian Lynx...

By the last of October, we had been in school for 5 or 6 weeks and it was time to let up on the kids and have a fun trip. I thought it would be great to take my classes on a picnic or weenie roast before cold weather was upon us. We went to the side of a lake that the kids talked about; close enough to town so that we could all hike. Everyone brought a lunch with cold cocoa in bottles or an orange crush soda; and cold boiled eggs and cookies.

It was a lovely sunny Saturday and everyone was happy. But --- what was I thinking? Taking all these kids into woods I knew nothing about? It was a reckless idea.

We all had a good time swapping sandwiches and one boiled egg for one large dill pickle, and trying each others' cup cakes. Kids always do this. We collected beautiful red leaves from the swamp maple trees and picked some late blooming asters.

At last, after a good day that had gone well, we packed up and headed out. I thought I knew the way, and off we trudged through the woods. Then we heard an ungodly piercing shriek from an animal that seemed right behind us. I pushed the kids hard to get out of those woods, and those shrieks followed us all the way. I was frantic, and horrified. The harder we ran, the louder that animal sounded. By now the kids had identified the animal as a Canadian Lynx and I made them run all the faster. Finally we came out of the woods on the road to town and spied a truck beside the road with the driver who pointed our way to town. I was relieved when we took count and knew everyone was safe. As for me, I was shaking like those birch tree leaves still on the trees. The entire adventure had scared me to death.

About a week later, I received a post card in the mail with a photograph of a Canadian Lynx on the other side. On the message side was this note:

*While on a weenie roast*

*A Canadian lynx came to drink a toast*

*And the graders cried*

*And the teacher sighed*

*Please, Mr. Lynx, leave us alone*

*And please, Mr. Thompson, take us home.*

The whole thing had been a put-up-job --- a big joke. There was no lynx or any other animal at all. Some high school boys had scared us all. They thought I was fair game --- a new young teacher in town. And the man in the pick-up truck? It was Mr. Thompson (whoever that was) and he was in on it, too.

I still have that post card since 1942, and more common sense now, I hope.

# Janet's Church Window Candy...

Melt:
1 - 6 ounce package of chocolate bits
¼ cup butter

Cool

Stir in:
3 cups miniature colored marshmallows
¼ cup nuts (optional)

Divide mixture into 2 logs

Roll in ½ cup chopped nuts and coconut

Wrap each log in waxed paper

Chill well and then  slice each log

I love this!

# Lice...

One day I spotted a real problem. When I was standing beside 7th grade Carolyn's desk where she was sitting, I could see bugs crawling all over her head; up and down and even side ways over her black hair. I thought she must be in agony. I knew I would have to do something about it. Since we did not have a school nurse, it was up to me to see that she got all those bugs out of her hair before every other kid in the room got their share of lice and they were all scratching at the same time. The only thing I could come up with was to have a little talk with Carolyn. She was a shy girl and I knew I should be very tactful and not hurt her feelings. That afternoon after school when all the kids had left except for Carolyn, I asked her if her long hair bothered her, and she broke into tears --- and of course, I almost cried too. I felt so sorry for her. She told me she had spoken to her mother about the lice but her mother hadn't done anything about it. I had heard somewhere that a shampoo with kerosene and a combing with a fine tooth comb would kill all the bugs, and I told her that. I told her how sorry I was, but she needed to have a clean head. She came to school the next morning all smiles and whispered to me, "They are all gone, Miss Kennedy." I wasn't sure of that but I knew the aroma was strong and our classroom smelled like a gasoline station. I guess word had gotten around, if not the lice, because half of the class reeked of greasy hair and kerosene, too.

Every day I found a new situation that had to be taken care of, hard feelings needed to be mended and kids needed to be encouraged, but I knew then that Carolyn needed some show of affection and I hugged her very tight.

# We Were So Cold...

One of my strongest memories of that northern Maine town was how <u>cold</u> it was. I made a promise to myself that I would never live north of Portland again. (Actually we did when we lived in Coos County in New Hampshire --- so much for idle promises.) We were so cold we could hear our boots as they crunched along on that icy road across <u>The Bridge</u>.

In the 1940's --- actually until the 1970's --- women teachers did not wear slacks in the classroom. Perish the thought! Since this school was drafty and cold, we swallowed our pride and sent to Sears Roebuck for those ugly brown thick cotton stockings --- the kind the pioneer women wore when they were on the covered wagons going out west in the 1850's. Those stockings had seams up the back that were always crooked with baggy wrinkles around the ankles. And, of course, we had to wear a girdle to hold the stockings up (if you never heard about girdles --- they are like corsets only a junior varsity number.) Isn't life pretty complicated when you make one decision --- wearing a girdle ---follows another --- wearing heavy stockings --- until you end up a different personality altogether? We even wore snuggies (warm underwear) to add to the whole shebang.

With all this added underpinning, we looked 20 pounds heavier than what we were, like fat old women plodding down the road to school with warm babushkas around our heads like immigrants right off the boat. Glamorous we weren't, but all this upholstery kept out those frigid winds blowing across the Androscoggin.

# German Peach Pie…

Arrange peach quarters in an unbaked pie shell

Mix together:
1 cup sugar
2 whole eggs
2 tbs. melted butter

Ladle over peaches in the pie shell

Sprinkle with
½ tsp. cinnamon
½ cup nutmeats

Bake 15 minutes in 425 degree oven

Reduce temperature to 350 degrees and bake an additional 45 minutes or until brown.

This is great and it is from Vermont

# The Halls...

We had wonderful landlords of our apartment upstairs over the Halls. They were a fine couple with 2 teenage kids. Mr. Hall had a rich baritone voice and the 4 of us often went downstairs in the evening to sing with him accompanied by his wife Mary at the piano. Seemed like a wild Saturday night in Northern Maine. Mr. Hall really cut loose on "There'll Always Be an England" and we would belt out the chorus. Anything British was great then; it was the jump-off place for our troops invading France or Germany (much later of course.) We were really good at that song but my great grandparents from Ireland would turn over in their graves to hear their grandson Frankie's daughter singing lustily about the country that had ruled them for so long and the country they had escaped from to come to the United States in the 1850's.

Back to the Halls. Since none of us girls knew how to start a wood fire in the kitchen stove and had no luck trying, Mr. Hall would come upstairs to our little kitchen early every morning to get the fire going before we got up.

At the time Doris had a boy friend in the Marines. When she heard he had gone AWOL (Away With Out Leave for younger people reading this) she was positive he would be heading up to Northern Maine to see <u>her</u>. Our imagination in this uninspiring town, in this dull school and in the hopeless war went on overtime and Doris convinced us that Phil would show up on our doorstep. We were sure the United States Marine Corps was after him and they would hand us off to the military prison in Leavenworth Kansas for aiding and abetting. The whole thing was pretty stupid on our part; how would he find Doris up here? and how would he get in?

One night when Doris was sure Phil would show up, we got prepared by putting milk bottles (milk bottles were all glass in those days) --- empty of course --- all over the kitchen floor, thinking that if Phil somehow got in and stumbled over those milk bottles in the dark, it would wake us all up. We didn't catch Phil, but we sure were startled when we heard Mr. Hall crashing over the bottles next morning when he yelled "What the hell is this?"

Doris never heard what happened to Phil for the next 40 years when he looked her up in Colorado. Too late for Phil --- Doris was married

# Mitzi's Peanut Butter Chocolate Bars...

Mix together:
2 cups crumbled chocolate cookie crumbs
½ cup melted butter

Press mixture into an 8" x 8" pan to make an even crust

Bake 10 minutes

Melt:
2 ½ cups of chocolate bits

Pour half of the chocolate over the crust; chill to firm the chocolate.

Mix together:
1 ½ cups creamy peanut butter
½ cup butter until smooth

Spread over chilled crust and chocolate.

Re-warm remaining chocolate and spread over peanut butter.

Chill until firm

# Maurice….

In the 7$^{th}$ grade sitting in the first row seat was Maurice, big for his age and usually tired. He was a good kid and no trouble, but impatient sometimes with school work that he thought was silly. I had been reading "The Midnight Ride of Paul Revere" to the class. It was just an easy ordinary - story type classic poem that every school kid knows. After a time of sitting quietly taking it all in, Maurice finally spoke his feelings, "I think this is a big waste of time for me, what good will it ever do me when I'm milking cows?" After searching for the right answer, I told him that nice poems like this would give him something pleasant to think about when he was working or milking cows. He shot back, "Not for me, the only thing

I think about when I'm milking those cows is making sure they don't stand on my feet.'

One day Maurice didn't finish his work and the rule was that kids had to stay after school to finish up. Maurice worked for a little while and when my back was turned, he lit out the door, and headed down the hill for home. No question, I ran right after him flat out as fast as I could. And I caught him, mostly because he was on the chubby side and at that time I was a fit 19 year old. I collared him and brought him back and he finished his work. I knew I had to catch him and follow through or he would never listen to me again.

Maurice and I were good friends after that and each of us respected the other. I respected him because he was an honest hard working farm kid; and he respected me because he knew I was fair and played by the rules.

# Peanut Butter Balls...

Combine:
2 boxes of confectioner's sugar
2 ½ cups peanut butter
1 lbs. soft butter or oleo
2 tsp. vanilla

Shape into small balls

Cool in fridge

Melt:
1 - 12 ounce package of chocolate bits
½ slab paraffin wax

Place the melted chocolate mixture over a pan of very hot water to keep it melted.

Stick balls with tooth picks and dip into melted chocolate

Be sure the chocolate mixture stays hot in order to keep dipping the peanut butter balls.

ANDROSCOGGIN RIVER

POND

WOODS

CANADIAN LYNX

N TO JAY

OUR HOUSE

IRON BRIDGE

LIVERMORE

S

ANDROSCOGGIN RIVER

DRUG STORE

BUS

RIVERSIDE SCHOOL

ME

LIVERMORE FALLS

TO LEWISTON

DIG DIG HOLES

SOUTH

LIVERMORE SCHOOL

1942

# Kennebunk
# 1943 – 1945

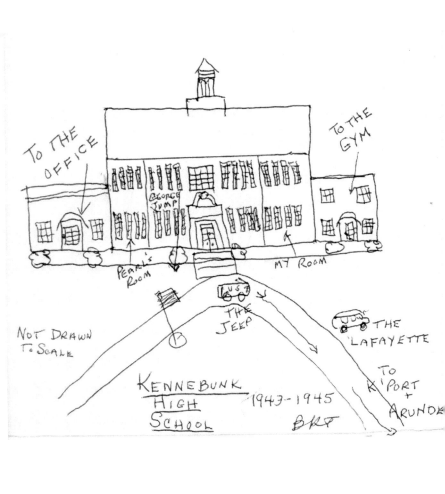

# Three

# My First Contract...

Well, I graduated from college and I was all cranked up to go "out in the field" as Doctor Bailey had put it a hundred times that I could remember. More like "fighting the good fight." Whatever. I wanted to do my best and it all came down to having a paycheck at last. I knew already just how I would spend it. The first thing would be a gorgeous pair of dark brown lizard pumps -- high heels of course. I would look like a professional working girl at least, like those classy ladies in the <u>Sunday New York Times</u>, in the <u>Style Section</u>,

It was during the summer when I was refinishing the dining room floor of my parents' house on Elm Street in North Berwick Maine. I looked like Popeye's Olive Oyl in the funny papers when Mr.

Carver, the Superintendent of Schools in the area, came to our house to discuss a job for me in Kennebunk. I never in my life looked any worse than I did that day; varnish all over my old clothes (that was before blue jeans) and varnish up to my armpits. I could not even shake hands with him. In spite of all that, he offered me a spot at Kennebunk High School, teaching social studies and civics in grades 7, 8 and 9. Just what I wanted! He said the job was mine for $1050 a year. It was $50 above the average for beginning teachers then. First he wanted me to meet the members of the school board. I could do that. Later that week I put on my navy blue dress that I was sure made me look older than I was --- 20. I went easy on the makeup and sashayed with all the confidence of my age to an evening meeting of the School Board at the Park Street School in Kennebunk. Mr. Carver introduced me to the three members whom I sized up in a minute flat. There was "Don" whose fuel oil company was advertised on the back of his work shirt in fancy stitched letters. Another man I was sure was a fisherman out of Cape Porpoise since "Don" asked him how the haddock were running. The third man, a coat and tie man, was probably an insurance agent whose business was printed on his tie clip which fastened his striped necktie to his shirt which stretched to the limit across his ample belly that was so big it had a life of its own and looked like it was old enough to vote. BUT very neat and small townish.

They asked me a lot of questions like, did I like kids? Oh yes I did. Could I handle a class of 30 high school kids? Oh yes, I could do that. I would say yes to any question they would ask. I wanted that job! The town of Kennebunk was a lovely town, the schools had an excellent rating, the subjects Social Studies and Civics were just what I liked and it was on the Coast where I wanted to be, just in case my Navy JG's ship the DE 258 came into Portland Navy Base (It did!)

Finally, Mr. Carver said to the Board, "Well boys, what do you think?" and the oil company man said "She looks pretty good to me." The other two men agreed, and I had my first contract.

Along with that, there were added attractions. My best friend Pearl would be the new science teacher, 2 doors down the hall from me. Beyond that, three friends in our college crowd would be teaching in York Beach 20 minutes away. It looked like we would be taking life at a pretty fast clip from then on.

# Pearl's Best Ever Lemon Meringue Pie...

Mix together and cook in a double boiler:
1 ¼ cups sugar
6 tbs. cornstarch
2 cups water

Mix together and add to sugar mixture:
1/3 cup lemon juice
3 eggs separated

Cook until thick about 25 minutes

Add:
3 tbs. butter
1 ½ tsp. lemon extract
2 tsp. vinegar

Stir thoroughly

Pour into cooked 9" pie shell

## MERINGUE

Blend:
1 tbs. cornstarch
2 tbs. cold water
½ cup boiling water

Cook stirring until clear and thickened

Let stand until completely cold

Beat together egg whites until foamy.

Gradually add 6 tbs. sugar and beat until stiff, not dry.

Turn mixer to low speed and add 1 tsp. vanilla

Gradually beat in cold cornstarch mixture

Turn mixer on high speed and beat well.

Spread over pie filling

Bake at 350 degrees for 10 minutes until meringue is light brown.

Pearl and I made this pie in Kennebunk in 1944.
It soothed our spirits after a hard day at KHS

# A Rap on the Knuckles...

Our principal at Kennebunk High School was one of the best. He was not a big man in stature, but he commanded great respect for the way he ran the high school. He was fair and every kid knew it. He moved all over that school, looked in on all our classes and checked the gym --- didn't have to say a word --- and the kids stayed in line. It took me a while to get used to the public address system, though. Mr. Allen could turn that little knob on the desk in his office, and tune in any place in the building and listen in. I was sure he was checking on me when I was losing an argument with an 8th grader. Then I realized he was checking up on the kids. He knew what kids were told to stay after school, what kids were late for class or what kids were disrupting classes.

In college, I was up to my eyeballs in Psychology and the spin was we would use all that psychology to figure out why a kid was a pain in the neck, why a kid answered back, or why a classroom could not be quieted down. Sounds good for psychology but no good. No one had actually discussed these problems and how to solve them. No one before had actually told us <u>what to do</u>. Every school had its own code of behavior and administration. I was fortunate to have an outstanding principal who had seen it all and gave us explicit suggestions how to handle problems that might arise. He gave us real choices; either rap the knuckles with a ruler (knuckle side up because it hurts more) or grab the kids' shoulders and give him a good shaking. Please remember, this is <u>1944</u>. I never used the ruler but I surprised some boys when I yanked them around a few times. I would have been in real trouble if the kid had yanked me back since he was almost double my size and almost my age as well. It only takes one or two situations like this to establish your reputation and claim respect. It really pleased me when Mr. Allen once in a while, would ask me to take charge of the double study hall --- 40 to 50 kids, because he thought I could handle it. And I did. I didn't like it but I did it.

Classroom behavior is more casual today. It beats me how a kid learns anything in today's free-for-all classrooms. It must be hard to get anything across to a class when everyone is talking and doing his own thing. My favorite news to my talkative students was "You are not learning when you are doing all the talking."

A good teacher must be knowledgeable in her subject and original in presenting it. That is the first requirement. But --- no matter how good her lessons are, she must know how to manage her classes and how to maintain strong discipline. I know behavior in modern schools is loose and casual but are the schools any better?

# Sour Cream Coffee Cake...

Cream together:
2 sticks of butter
2 cups of sugar
4 eggs

In separate bowl, mix:
4 cups flour
2 tsp. baking powder
2 tsp. baking soda
Then mix all together

Add:
1 pt. sour cram
The batter will be heavy and stiff

In a small bowl mix:
1 cup sugar
1 cup chopped walnuts
2 tsp. cinnamon

Grease and flour a round pan, angel food pan or Bundt pan

Plop half the mixture into baking pan

Sprinkle with half the nut mix

Plop the rest of the batter into pan and sprinkle with rest of walnut mix on top.

Bake 1 hour in at 350 degree oven

If the top is browning too quickly, cover cake with aluminum foil

Cake is done when it sounds hollow on top
You want the cake to be done but not overdone as it is best when it is moist.

This coffee cake is one of the very best.

# This Was a Jeep...

This was 1943 --- wartime --- when Pearl and I were teaching in Kennebunk. The war affected everyone's daily living. For us, we took part in selling war bonds (not many) and stamps (a lot) every Thursday at school, as did all the staff. There was a lot of competition in this --- sometimes with special prizes. One "War Bond Day", a new jeep from one of the forts in Portland with 2 young soldiers (of course they were young --- every soldier was!) came to our school.

Jeeps were a product of the war, and not many people had had a first person look at one, and no one had ever had a <u>ride</u> in one. These 2 soldiers were at our school giving rides to the kids who had bought the most defense stamps that day. Since Pearl and I were the youngest teachers on the staff, it is believable that the soldiers wanted to take us for a ride --- literally. They gave Mr. Allen a dozen reasons why Miss Hartt and Miss Kennedy should go for a spin in the jeep. Mr. Allen said he would take over our homerooms, and the Jeep hit the road with 2 soldiers and 2 young teachers who loved adventure. All we needed was a marching band ahead of us. It was a lovely sunny morning in May and this was pretty good duty for the soldiers, and a nice change from the classrooms for Pearl and me. We sped all the way to Kennebunkport and Arundel and all points in between. I loved the ride but I was getting nervous thinking of Mr. Allen taking over our classes while we were out for a joy ride. When we finally arrived at school we said thanks a bunch to the soldiers and then we apologized to Mr. Allen who didn't seem a bit surprised that we had been gone so long. C'est le guerre!

# Butterscotch Meringue Pie...

<u>CRUST</u>

Combine:
1 1/3 cups graham cracker crumbs (about 20 crackers)
6 tbs. melted butter
¼ cup sugar

Press crust mixture firmly over bottom and sides of 9" pan

Bake 8 minutes at 350 degrees. Do not over bake

Cool before filling

<u>FILLING</u>

Scald 2 cups milk in double boiler over hot water.

In a bowl mix:
1 cup brown sugar
¼ tsp. salt
6 tbs. flour

Using a whisk, stir in hot milk

Return mixture to pan and continue simmering and stirring over hot water until thickened. Stir a ladle full of milk mixture into 3 beaten egg yokes, and then add the egg mixture to custard in the pan. Simmer until well thickened.....about 8 minutes more.

Cool

## MERINGUE

Beat until stiff:
3 egg whites
¼ tsp. cream of tartar
6 tbs. sugar

Fill crust with butterscotch custard

Cover with meringue

Bake at 425 degrees for about 5 minutes

# Cora B...

The other members of the staff were very cordial to us, especially Cora Littlefield who had been teaching school for years and years. She was in her 60's I guess, and very lame, but let me tell you she could handle those kids with the <u>Look</u>, and they would jump to do her bidding. She was an excellent teacher and the kids liked her. They didn't even try to get out of line in her room. She was very kind to Pearl and me, beginning teachers with her classroom between Pearl's and mine. I'll bet she cringed more than once to observe our methods of teaching.

One lucky day all classes in grades 7 and 8 went into the auditorium to see a film. I can't remember what it was of course, but probably some winner about using the dictionary or maybe the habits of a garden snake. As we were filing out of the auditorium, Miss Littlefield came to my side and said very quietly as if she were giving me the password to open the vault at the bank, "Miss Kennedy, one of your students, Kenneth Day, was chewing gum all though the film." I of course, thanked her, but I sure didn't care if the entire crowd chewed bubble gum and blew bubbles with it in the darkness of that film showing. Why stir up a hornet's nest when we don't need to? And if the gum made that film more palatable, so be it. I left Kenneth alone.

# Candy's Williamsburg Trifle...

1 pkg. yellow cake mix
1 - 16 ounce pkg. frozen strawberry halves --- thawed
1 pkg. vanilla pudding made according to package directions
1 cup chilled whipping cream
¼ cup sugar
¼ cup tasted slivered almonds
5 whole strawberries or cherries

Bake cake mix in 13" x 9" pan as directed on the package.
Cut the cake in half crosswise (freeze one half for future use.)
Split each piece horizontally. Arrange half the pieces in 2 quart glass serving bowl, cutting pieces to fit the bowl.
Pour half the thawed strawberries over cake in the bowl. Spread with half of the pudding. Repeat and cover.
Chill at least 8 hours.
Beat cream until stiff; spread over trifle.
Sprinkle with almonds, garnish with strawberries or cherries.

# George --- the Class Clown...

George, a large size senior, had been a trial for the new English teacher (not me.) Somehow they didn't get along. George was a nice average 18 year old and known as the class clown doing outrageous things to make the other students laugh. He was very disruptive in her English class all the time. It was for sure that her lessons on participles, infinitives and similes were pretty dull and boring to these boys who would be going into the army after graduation.

Finally, this teacher couldn't put up with George any more that day so she put him in the book closet in the back of her room on the second floor. It left her class in peace and she thought it was great. George was in that closet with a couple hundred books. He was very quiet; probably entranced by one of those books in there like an out-of-date Britannica Encyclopedia.

At the end of the class, after her group had left, the teacher opened the door to let George out of solitary. But George wasn't in there. That teacher was scared to death; she knew the principal would not approve of the disappearance of one of her class, right under her very eyes. She was a wreck. Then she realized the window in the closet was open. George had flown the coop! He had used the design of the exterior bricks for foot holds down the front of that building until he got to the ground floor --- and then he jumped. He came out a hero to the kids, of course. After graduation, George joined the United States Marine Corps. He had a head start on scaling walls. It was a cinch for George.

# Margaret's Apple Walnut Cake...

Combine and let stand:
4 cups chopped apples
2 cups sugar

Beat together:
2 eggs
2 tsp. vanilla
½ cup oil

Stir together:
2 tsp. soda
2 tsp. cinnamon
1 tsp. salt
1 cup chopped walnuts

Mix all together with apples and sugar

Pour into a greased and floured 13" x 9" pan.

Bake 1 hour at 350 degrees

## FROSTING

Mix:
5 tbs. butter
3 cups confectionary sugar
2 tbs. lemon juice
1 or 2 tbs. cold water

# We Kept Up…

When we were teaching at Kennebunk our armed forces were in battles all over the world. These kids had members of their families in the Service and they were interested in keeping up with the news. Eisenhower was in Europe; MacArthur in the Pacific and FDR was in the White House. The classes and I kept maps on our walls up-to date. After the allied invasion of Italy and France on June 6, 1944 we plotted on our large map of Europe just where our troops were. It made these kids listen carefully to the radio and read the papers, and they did. Some of the kids hustled right into my classroom every morning so they could fill in (with chalk) just where the troops had fought. It meant a lot to these kids, 60 years later in 2005, I met a former student of mine and after he introduced me to his wife said to her, "She's the one who let us keep up with the Invasion by marking her map on the wall."

Those two years teaching at Kennebunk High School were great for me. As I entered my first classroom in 1943 I was no longer a student; I was <u>The Teacher</u>. I knew I had a great responsibility, facing these kids every day and being part of their lives. I made an earnest attempt at both teaching and learning and I always tried to find something to laugh about..

# Judy's Miniature Cheesecakes...

Place one Nabisco Nilla Wafer in each cupcake paper in a muffin tin.

## FILLING

Beat together until smooth:
2 – 8 ounce pkgs. cream cheese
3 eggs
½ cup sugar
1 tsp. vanilla

Pour over wafers

Bake 350 degrees for 15 - 20 minutes

After baking top each cupcake with cherry pie filling, 3 or 4 cherries for each cupcake.

Makes 1 ½ to 2 dozen

# The Lafayette...

Pearl and I had 2 great years at Kennebunk. We had an apartment together on Grove Street. Pearl loved to cook and was good at it, too. I loved everything she made; especially her lemon meringue pie, but I could not enjoy beef heart. Not for me. I stuck to American Chop Suey.

At that time Pearl had her mother's car --- a huge noisy old black Lafayette. It was low slung with wooden spoke wheels. It had big headlights, painted black half way down the lens for blackout reasons. It made that car look like a large size Dracula, with half closed eyes, big, black and bold. Somehow Pearl had broken off the key in the ignition and every time she tried to start the car she had to fit the remaining half of the key into the part that was trapped forever in the ignition. Sometimes it was easy to connect, but usually it took a while to fit those keys together. Whenever we went anywhere we had to allow extra time to get the old tank moving.

Pearl was the girls' high school basketball coach. Her teams were champions in Maine. In those days, the team rode in the coach's car. One night, when she was going to drive to a game in York, I was watching Pearl out the window when she was having a fit, trying to get that car going. As I watched her, I heard the sports announcer of a Portland radio station say, "Tonight the champion Kennebunk team will travel to York to play…." And I stood there laughing and shaking my head thinking "they will if Pearl can get the Lafayette moving."

Not long after that Pearl and I planned a weekend in York Beach with our college buddies, Ginnie and Barbara and Rachel. We loaded food and suitcases on the back seat and lashed our bikes to the sides of the car. Pearl and I made a smashing arrival at their place in York Beach. Along their front yard was a pretty white picket fence; and Pearl, not allowing space on the sides of the car for our bicycles, picked off every single white picket with a loud plink, plink, plink and that was the end of that fence, but the tough old Lafayette could run for another thousand miles.

# Pearl's Cherry Pie...

For 9" pie, drain 2 - 16 ounce cans of pitted red tart cherries.

Line a 9" pie plate with pastry

Mix together:
1 1/3 cup sugar
1/3 cup flour

Stir in cherries

Turn into pastry lined pan.

Sprinkle with ¼ tsp. almond extract

Dot with butter

Cover with top crust that has slits cut in it; seal and flute

Cover edge with strip of aluminum to prevent excessive browning

Bake at 425 degrees for 35 – 45 minutes.

Remove the foil during last 15 minutes of baking.
Bake until crust is brown and juice begins to bubble through slits in crust

Wonderful!

# Pickles at the Opera…

We had some wonderful weekends away from our teaching. Several times we joined our York Beach crowd for trips to Boston to hear Lily Pons at the Symphony Hall, the Ice Follies at the Boston Garden and the opera <u>Tannhauser</u>. That adventure leaves me embarrassed to think about. One Saturday the 5 of us took the bus to Boston and had no time to eat, so we brought our tuna sandwiches and dill pickles with us to the opera house. We were careful not to make any noisy crinkle of the waxed paper and we only took bites of our pickles during the loud music, as well as chewing very quietly during the romantic part. We were probably the only opera goers at the performance keeping time to Wagner's opera with dill pickles.

But --- after a while we heard comments like "What's that I smell? from an opera goer with her jeweled bosom and her blue hair. After that we chewed fast while the fat lady sang.

Later that winter Pearl had planned to spend the weekend in Boston at the Massachusetts College of Pharmacy with handsome Charlie. She had been getting ready for a month. Two days before she would take the bus to Boston, her face swelled double its size, and there was no doubt about it, she had MUMPS in a big way --- on both sides of her jaws. Of course, she decided she would go to Boston, anyway. She wore high collar outfits and pulled her hair down around her face. She said she kept her face dipped down in a flirty way all weekend. No one commented and she had a marvelous time. She never knew whether that college had an outbreak of mumps after that or not. I suspect they did because she never heard from Charlie again.

# Chocolate Sheet Cake...

Preheat oven to 375 degrees

Coat a jelly roll pan with cooking spray and dust with 2 tsp. flour

Combine in large bowl:
2 cups flour
2 cups sugar
1 tsp. baking soda

Combine in sauce pan:
¾ cup water
½ cup butter
¼ cup cocoa

Bring to a boil, stirring frequently

Remove from heat. Pour into flour mixture

Beat together until well blended

Add:
½ cup buttermilk or plain milk with 1 tsp. vinegar
1 tsp. vanilla
2 large eggs
Beat well

Pour batter into prepared pan. Bake at 375 degrees for 17 minutes. Place on a wire rack to cool.

## ICING

Bring to boil in a sauce pan and stir constantly:
6 tbs. butter
1/3 cup milk
¼ cup cocoa

Remove from heat and gradually stir in:
3 cups powdered sugar
¼ cup pecan or walnuts
2 tsp. vanilla

Spread over hot cake.

Makes 20 servings

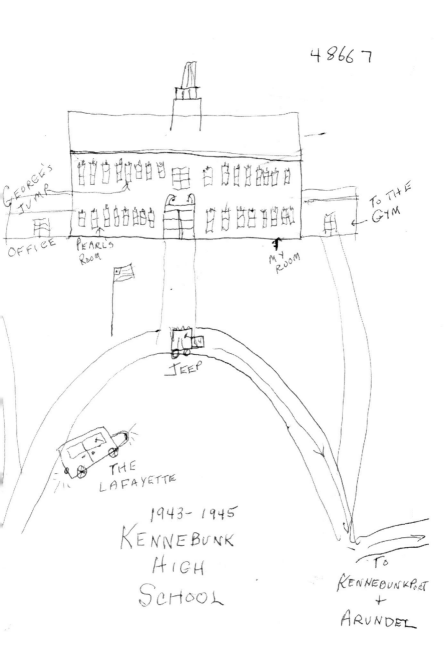

48667

GEORGE'S JUMP

TO THE GYM

OFFICE

PEARL'S ROOM

MY ROOM

JEEP

THE LAFAYETTE

1943 - 1945
KENNEBUNK
HIGH
SCHOOL

TO KENNEBUNKPORT + ARUNDEL

# North Berwick
# 1949-1950

# Four

# My Banner Year...

In 1949 the new North Berwick High School on High Street opened for the first time. It had 4 years of high school and the 8th grade. I was happy to be the new 8th grade teacher. Harry Truman was in the White House, General McArthur was in Korea and Bill Reagan was principal of our school.

I had substituted in this grade in the past and I had been very strict. A sub's job is to keep the kids in line with a firm hand because the kids will really try to make her life miserable just for the fun of it. So this 8th grade was ready to hate me. Fortunately it turned out happily for them and for me. They have been my favorite class through it all. This was my home town and I had to do well.

We read Johnny <u>Tremain</u> and learned about the American Revolution; and we heard of <u>King of the Wind</u> about a little Arabian horse. I always liked to read to my classes. I knew if they could enjoy a book read to them they had a good chance to read on their own. In 2005, at a fair at Union Maine, I saw a beautiful Arabian horse being shown. As I admired it, I mentioned to the owner how it reminded me of the book, <u>King of the Wind</u> and she grinned and said "Oh yes, yes, I read that --- wasn't that a wonderful story?" Reading opens up a whole new way of life, and I stressed good books in my class.

There were 20 kids in that class; 10 boys and 10 girls. They were all wonderful kids; not a problem of any kind. There was a strong feeling of camaraderie among them and for me. These 8th graders of 1949 and 1950 are grandparents now; a few gray heads and a few stylish stouts. It has tickled me to death to be included in their alumni reunions. Two years ago in 2004 this class of North Berwick High School had its 50th reunion and they still laughed at all my jokes and remembered all those books we read. I have been very proud of the life success of them all.

I can't remember the courses I taught that year. I suppose we studied parts of speech in English class, percentages in math --- (only we called it arithmetic then,) spelling, the rivers of Maine and in current events we studied the members of the Supreme Court and learned about the President's Cabinet. I am sure we did all that, I can't remember those subjects but I can remember every single one of those kids and their faces.

And here they are ---

| | |
|---|---|
| Patsy | Sylda |
| Sonny | Roger |
| Geraldine | Diane |
| Bob | Paul |
| Jean | Marlene |
| Bruce | Timothy |
| Ann | Elizabeth |
| Eddie | Bobby |
| Sandra | Priscilla |
| Malcolm | Gordon |

# Caramel Corn...

Pop 6 quarts of pop corn

In a saucepan:
Melt 1 cup butter or oleo
Add ½ cups light Karo syrup
2 cups light brown sugar
½ tsp. salt

Let bubble 3 minutes. Do not stir

Turn off heat and add ½ tsp. vanilla

Pour hot syrup over pop corn mixing well with large cooking fork

Place in 2 baking pans Bake 225 degrees for 1 hour After 15 minutes, mix through the pop corn, then again 15 minutes later

Cool and enjoy.

*Great fun for kids to make!*

# I Had a Crisis of My Own...

As a teacher I was always working kids through one crisis or another, but in 1949 I had one of my own. Even though I was only 27 years old and a size 12, I wore a girdle like every other female did. You know what a girdle is: it's a light weight junior model of a corset. I don't know where the line is drawn between them but the girdle was only worn to keep our stockings up without bagging around the ankles. If the girdle came in a medium size a little support for the back side was thrown in. No panty hose then. I wore a rubber girdle which was like a second skin and I thought it gave me a wonderful line, smoothed out the wrinkles and bulges and made me look a size or two slimmer. One morning when I was walking to school on High Street, a high school senior,

Lisle Eaton, stopped to give me a ride which I always thought was great. Not this time, though. When I climbed into that car I could feel that rubber girdle giving way completely up the side. I knew the whole apparatus would soon be down around my ankles, garters, stockings and all at any moment. Not a very good start for that day that would ever be remembered as "The day Mrs. Tufts' underwear gave way." And the jokes would get funnier and funnier for everyone but me. I had to think fast. When we arrived at school, I told Lisle not to move --- just stay in the car until I came back. I took the backdoor, walking as carefully as I could, feeling that girdle creeping halfway down my knees.

When I got into Mr. Reagan's office I told him I needed to go back home for something and would he cover my class and also allow Lisle to be a little late? Bill said "It sounds like a crisis to me, but go ahead." My pride was saved and no one was the wiser when I came back to school a half hour later with another way to hold up my stockings. I saw Lisle the other day --- I think he's 74-75 years old now and he said he always wondered what my crisis was back in 1949 but he didn't dare ask.

# Sheila's Divinity Fudge...

Boil together:
2 cups granulated sugar
½ cup dark Karo
½ cup water
¼ tsp. salt

Beat until stiff 2 egg whites with electric mixer, then carefully add the sugar mixture slowly, beating with the mixer.

When it is fudge- like, pour into greased pan to harden.

Cut into squares.

# Sonny...

Sonny was a red headed boy in our 8th grade. He was full of fun and could make everyone in the class laugh while seeming to be very well behaved himself. The girls all loved him but he didn't realize that (then.) He was just happy to be part of the crowd. He was a good student but he was a spelling inventor, sometimes spelling the same word 3 different ways in one paragraph. He made his own choices of spelling. Before their weekly spelling test sometimes I would tell the class that I would give them each a candy bar if every single one of them got 100 on the test. That was 1950 and no one would frown on that then, either for bribery or all that sugar. Well, the kids coached Sonny all week studying those words.

Somehow we all knew the candy would not come their way, and it never did.

During that year I had a conversation with Sonny's father. He said, "I don't know what the matter is with that kid. The girls came over to our house every night to study and do homework. When the girls get ready to go home it's dark and I always ask Sonny if he's going to walk the girls home. Of course, he never does, but the girls keep coming over. I don't know what's wrong with him!" Sonny just wasn't ready to walk anyone home --- but he learned soon enough.

# We Went to the City...

That year those 8th graders did well. I had them for all classes except for Industrial Arts for the boys. This class was easy to handle --- only got loud and noisy sometimes --- well, actually a lot --- but they would quiet down when I spoke to them.

I promised them a trip to Boston in the spring and those kids earned money and saved it all winter. The School Board allowed us to use a school bus and a driver and we had 2 or 3 mothers join us.

We climbed Bunker Hill, went aboard <u>Old Ironsides</u>, watched all the activities in Boston Harbor and went to a museum at Harvard University. I took them to a real Scandinavian Smorgasbord restaurant for their dinner. That stopped them cold: whether they liked the food or not they ate it anyway and talked about it all the way home. The herring in the sour cream, the ham in raisin sauce and the raspberry salad. I thought they were pushing it a little too much, talking about all that food when one of the boys had been carsick on the way up. (Not to worry, our bus driver just pulled up to a clothing store where our boy bought a new sweater.) So on the way home I thought it was ill-advised to talk about any food, let alone the strange Swedish fare, but they had seen the world that day!

# Favorite Fudge…

Mix:
2 cups sugar
¾ cups evaporated milk

Add:
2 - 1 ounce squares unsweetened chocolate melted
1 tsp corn syrup (Karo)

Bring to a boil --- stirring often

Test for doneness by dropping a teaspoonful into a cup of cold water. It is done when the drop of fudge clings together like a ball.

Remove from the stove

Add and beat together:
Dash of salt
2 tbs. butter
1 tsp. vanilla

Keep beating as it cools and until it feels like it is hardening.

Pour into a square pan and let cool completely
This is fun to make on a rainy day or a dull Sunday afternoon.

# Pennsylvania
# 1950 – 1951

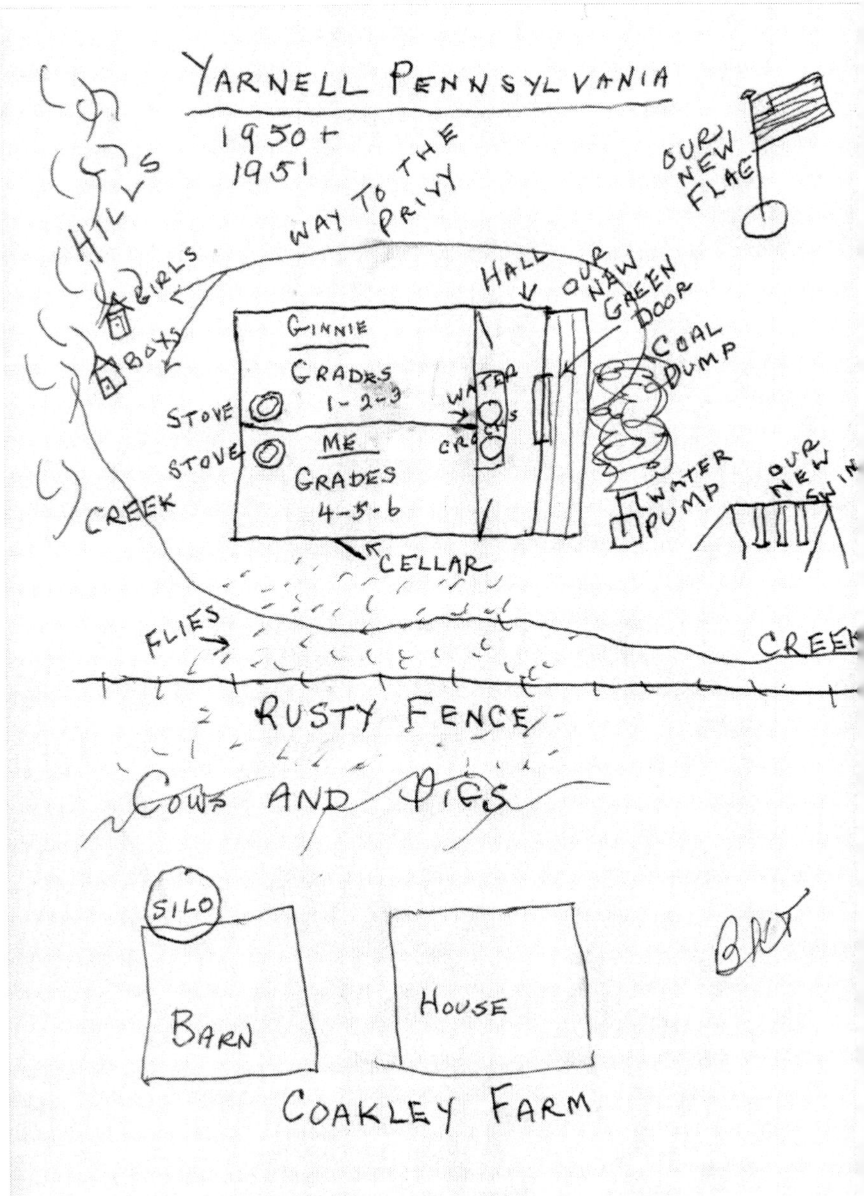
YARNELL PENNSYLVANIA
1950 + 1951
HILLS
WAY TO THE PRIVY
GIRLS
BOYS
OUR NEW FLAG
HALL
OUR NEW GREEN DOOR
COAL DUMP
GINNIE
GRADES 1-2-3
STOVE
STOVE
ME
GRADES 4-5-6
WATER
CREEK
WATER PUMP
OUR NEW SWIN
CELLAR
FLIES
CREE
RUSTY FENCE
COWS AND PIGS
SILO
BARN
HOUSE
COAKLEY FARM

HILLS

HILLS

ROAD

LITTLE CHURCH

PIGS

To ART's + MABEL's HOUSE

Us

MILLER'S HOUSE

MR. MILLER'S STORE

CREEK

PIGS' ROAD TRIP

MAIN ROAD

MILESBURG

BELLEFONTE

PENN STATE

NOT DRAWN TO SCALE

# Five

# The Plan...

In 1950 Stan and I and our 4 year old daughter Candy went to live in Centre County Pennsylvania while Stan went to graduate school at Penn State. We made great plans with our old friends, Ginnie and Neal Ward who went along with us. Our intentions were that Stan and Neal would drive to State College every day and Ginnie and I would teach school --- if we got jobs. The 6 of us would live together and find a baby sitter for Candy and Linda, their 2 year old daughter. Sounds impossible, but we did it.

The 4 of us went down to Pennsylvania the summer before school started to make arrangements for our great <u>PLAN.</u> After Stan and Neal were all set with their college courses, Ginnie and I went to the Centre County School office in

Bellefonte to see if the County was dying to hire 2 Maine teachers for a couple of their classrooms. When we heard that the County superintendent was at an evening meeting in the next town, that's where we went to look him up. He was a smallish man with a skinny moustache under his nose like William Powell in the movies. He, the county superintendent (not William Powell) hustled out from his meeting to talk with Ginnie and me in the hallway. Five minutes later we were hired to teach in a 2 room school up in the hills. Ginnie would have grades 1, 2 and 3 while I had grades 4, 5 and 6. We took a chance on that school and they took a chance on us. Mr. Shaw gave us directions how to get to the school on the back side of the mountains and told us the key to the school was at a neighbor's house where we could pick it up. So much for a welcoming committee.

We were all pumped up to go out over those mountains to find that little settlement of Yarnell and look over the school we had committed ourselves to, now that we had signed the contracts. Had we jumped too soon? Where was this school anyway? We were a little suspicious about the whole thing. Why hadn't they signed up teachers for that school long before this, the middle of August?

Reaching Yarnell, we found a little group of houses, maybe 6 or 7, and one store that sold only bread, milk and RED MAN CHEWING TOBACCO, plus gasoline from one gasoline pump. A one room church was nearby, neatly cared for.

At last we came across a sad little schoolhouse that seemed like it had been overlooked by the Civil War. This was the Yarnell School --- away from the road and clinging for dear life to the side of a good size hill. The school was one story with 2 classrooms and a hallway between. When I went through the entrance, double doors --- filthy and worn --- for the first time, I knew I would have to paint them. No way could I pass through those doors every day without hating them, the school, Yarnell, Centre County, Pennsylvania and the automobile that brought me here. Those doors would discourage anyone from going inside. A week later I bought my own can of paint --- a strong and brave shade of green and slapped it on the doors. Everyone liked it, especially me. It sort of gave that old building a little authority. Not much, but some.

On one side of the school house was a bubbling creek (the kids corrected me --- it was a <u>crick</u>) free running and clean, over a few rocks. It was 4 feet wide and maybe 12 inches deep, but it was wet and a big attraction for the kids. We would soon find out that the creek was a big nuisance when we hauled kids out of that cold water every other day. The boy --- wringing wet --- enjoyed all the attention of the other kids when he had to roll up his pant legs, take off his shoes and stockings all dripping wet and drape them over the top of the STOVE where they steamed and smelled all afternoon. I bawled out the kids every time someone fell into the water and threatened all kinds of stuff if they did it again. They were a little more careful, but not much.

Back to the STOVES; each room had its own.  Actually they were <u>furnaces</u> burning wood and coal and each one had a "jacket" around it. These battered and bent steel jackets were high and curved around the stoves, preventing anyone from falling onto a hot stove. I found these jackets handy for a lot of other reasons. They were great for drying out wet clothes and heating water for washing hands. We paid a 6th grade boy to start the fires every school day. These kids knew all about furnaces, stoves, and kindling. They kept those fires going; they threw in a hod full of coal every now and then all day; they seemed to know just when. They did it with a proud swagger, knowing more about keeping a fire going than the teachers did. I learned more than I ever wanted to know about coal fires and dampers. I figured if I ever got out of this school I would never take on a school again that didn't have a working thermostat on the wall. Ginnie was not so lucky; since she had just little kids --- grades 1, 2 and 3, she had to keep her own fires going. 3rd graders just cannot throw a hod full of coal into a yawning fire. It soon showed on Ginnie's bosom because every dress or sweater she owned had two big round blobs of coal dust on her generous chest!

At one time in the fall, our coal and wood supply got very low and we had burned up everything we could find in the cellar including old desks and broken chairs. We even burned up 2 old Christmas trees which I am sure had been in the cellar since Calvin Coolidge left the White House. The spills were gone but still clinging to the branches were old paper chains that some kiddo had made a long time ago.

Stan and Neal stopped in at the County Superintendent's office and spoke loudly about our fuel situation. It got results all right, only our new supply of coal was dumped right smack in front of the entrance steps of the schoolhouse with our nice new green door. If you have lemons you make lemonade; right then we turned it into a game. We gave the 5th and 6th graders a chance to make a trail through the coal. The kids just loved it; sort of like Tom Sawyer getting his fence white washed.

We felt pretty fortunate that our coal had arrived when we heard that the Red Roost School down the mountain from us got a load of hard wood for fuel and a new ax for splitting it up. How lucky could we be? Shows you right there the gold plated importance that we had in that school district.

# Calico Beans...

Sauté and brown in a large pan...
½ lb. bacon until crisp

Remove bacon. Save fat in pan

Sauté 6 sliced onions in fat and add to bacon

Mix together...
½ cup brown sugar
¼ cup vinegar
½ cup chili sauce
1-teaspoon mustard
Toss in with bacon and onions.

Add...
1 can Campbell's beans and tomato sauce
1 can lima beans
1 can butter beans
1 can kidney beans
Do not drain the beans

Stir all together and simmer. Do no let the beans get mushy.

I have this in another recipe collection, but since it is so good, I have added it here!

# Mr. Miller...

Now that Ginnie and I had jobs in Yarnell, we had to find a place for all of us to live. We started in the neighborhood of our school and the 4 of us took turns knocking on doors. We had no luck until we drove by a large asphalt shingled house with an old man rocking away his afternoon on the front porch, minding his own business. It was Neal's turn --- and with Neal's downeast powers of persuasion he talked his way into the man's (Mr. Miller) favor, and we had our new residence for the next school year. Mr. Miller charged each couple $10 a month.

It took a lot of courage for 74 year old Mr. Miller to take in 2 strange couples and 2 little girls. He didn't know any of us when we moved in bag and baggage in September of 1950. We just about took over the house with Ginnie and I doing the cooking and cleaning. We had a great system worked out. One week Stan and I would plan the meals and do the cooking while Ginnie and Neal did the cleaning up, the next week we reversed the whole operation. Mr. Miller took all his supper meals with us and he told the neighbors that those Maine girls put onions in everything --- and he didn't understand why we baked beans every Saturday --- just BEANS.

Mr. Miller was crotchety at times and he couldn't imagine why Ginnie and I did so much cleaning. I went so far as to wrap aluminum foil around his old peach cans with droopy and sad plants in them. He had them in every window, sagging with the weight of the coal dust that spread over everything in the room. Right then and there I knew that coal dust had taken over my life.

Mr. Miller complained when we used his washing machine which hadn't been plugged in for fifteen years. Using that 1928 Maytag was no fun. The rubber on the wringers leaked thick black grease on one side. That took some sensitive care with the Fruit of the Looms. Plus we had Mr. Miller underfoot trying to discourage us from using that pesky wringer. Then when we realized how ridiculous the whole operation was, Ginnie and I nearly killed ourselves laughing, and that made all the difference.

For a while Stan and Neal had a late class on Friday nights, so Ginnie and I did the laundry that night, keeping our weekends free for our wild social life; playing Canasta recklessly and eating chocolate cake frosted with a foot of smooth chocolate fudge. Actually we did show up for the inaugural ball at the University when Doctor Milton Eisenhower (Ike's brother) became president of Penn State. It was a pretty swanky event and we really dolled up for the affair. No one could ever know of the coal dust living we had in Yarnell. No one would know how often we had been invited to a hog butchering. We never went, but several times we were presented with a yard of home made sausage on Monday morning. Another pastime that my 6th grade boys bragged about was "burning cars." Their fathers collected old junky cars which they burned up every Saturday night and offered liquid refreshment of hard cider for their guests.

Back to the washing on Friday nights. Ginnie usually made doughnuts that night and it created a tough decision for Mr. Miller to make; whether to be mad about our using his washing machine on a Friday night at 9 o'clock or sit up late to eat

2 or 3 hot doughnuts dunked in sugar. He loved those doughnuts.

Mr. Miller maintained a grudge at any customer who stopped at his store for groceries; you know I already told you he only sold bread and milk and chewing tobacco or gasoline at the one pump. I never knew what kind he sold --- was it regular or was it high test? But he didn't care either way --- he only sold one kind.

There were 2 big stoves in the house; the parlor stove was a big size fancy number from Sears Roebuck that took bucket after bucket of coal from the bin outside. The house had no cellar where Maine people were smart enough to keep their coal. That parlor stove was also where Mr. Miller spit his tobacco juice in a lengthy stream from his cheeks. He did this with a great system --- he just opened that stove door, put his head for forceful spitting and let her go. From my place at the eating/cooking/studying table I had a direct line of vision to that big old parlor stove and the flying tobacco juice. Sometimes, it killed my appetite.

The kitchen stove was the center of operations. Every night when Mr. Miller went to bed he banked the fire in that stove for the night. It made the kitchen really freezing for us to sit around the table while Stan and Neal did their heavy duty studying or Ginnie and I prepared our lessons. Not to worry, the guys threw in buckets of coal which warmed us up in no time. In the morning Mr. Miller would say he couldn't understand why the fire burned up so fast.

Mr. Miller was not the huggable type and his chuckles were as rare as a nickel with the buffalo going the wrong way, but looking back 60 years ago, I wonder how he could stand us, 4 adults and 2 little girls. He did well to open his house and give us a home for that year, and I'll bet that he talked about those Maine people for the rest of his life.

# Candy's Broccoli Soup...

Cook until tender 1 – 10 ounce pkg. chopped broccoli

Put in blender with cooking water.

Blend well, adding
½ to 1 chicken bouillon cube

Dump into sauce pan

Add 1 can cream of mushroom soup diluted with
½ - 1 cup light cream

Spoon some sour cream over the tops of serving dishes.

Candace Crawford

# Mabel...

We got lucky when we found Mabel to take care of our little girls, Candy, 4 years old and Linda who was 2 ½. Mabel had never married and she lived with her brother Art on the home place just around the mountain. Art was single too, and they both were in their late 60s I guess. They just loved our girls and we thought Mabel and Art spent most of their time entertaining them on the farm. One night after school I drove down there to pick them up and each little girl bounced into the back seat with a sputtering angry hen under her arms. Mabel said she couldn't stand to take away the hens because Linda and Candy had been playing with them all day. Lucky hens!

Sometimes Mabel came to our house to look after the girls. That must have been a wild time for Mabel --- balancing the girls on one hand and keeping Mr. Miller happy on the other hand. The neighbors wondered if Mabel and Mr. Miller would take up with each other. Nope, it never happened.

It was a fun place on the farm for the girls. It was an old fashion place, hens and chickens, an old goat showing his age in spite of the special care he received, and one lonesome cow. They had a spring house where they kept food cool, and a small barn full of hay where they kept the cow and goat.

Mabel and Art were dear sweet people. Art had been in World War I, an Army private, and returned to the farm, put on his overalls and had stayed there at home ever since. Mabel had stayed there too, and had once been on a church ladies' bus trip to Washington, D.C. and that had been enough for her. We were truly blessed to have this trim little lady with snow white hair taking care of the 2 little girls.

# Carrot and Apple Casserole...

Spread cooked carrots in a buttered casserole

Over the carrots spread one can of apple filling.

Then spread over all:
brown sugar
cinnamon
nutmeg
little ginger
butter

Then brown in the oven.

A New Hampshire school teacher served this at a luncheon I attended.

# Running Water...

No piped in water in this school --- just a hand pump located outdoors by the front steps. Why in the world was the pump put in the yard instead of <u>inside </u>the building? Someone thought he was doing a great favor to the world by putting in the pump right beside the front door --- easy to get to in all kinds of weather, someone thought.

We dug around down there in that moldy cellar  where we found an old bench, 2 heavy water crocks, and 20 pencils those kids had accidently on purpose pushed down through the cracks and holes in the floor of the classroom. (Truly those cracks were a quarter inch wide.) The kids made great sport of this until I realized they loved having a little stroll outside and down into the cellar to collect their pencils. After a couple of days of this, I made a list of daily pencil collectors whose job it was to pick up those pencils in that damp trashy cellar. That job was a killer because the cellar smelled like the dump, but the kids thought it was neat  to have that job posted on the wall with their names on the list.

Back to the water supply. We brought up the crocks with spigots on the sides and put one in each classroom on an empty desk. It didn't do any damage to those desks because the bottoms of them were missing anyway. The older boys filled up the crocks every morning and then we had running water; running down the aisles or running under the desks when we couldn't close the spigots tight enough. Or maybe the kids just let them go, just to create a little action. So, we put the old bench we had found down cellar into the front hall and told the kids to bring in their own cups for their drinks. I knew Centre County School District would never spring for paper cups. So with my trusty hammer I put 30 nails in 2 rows right on the hall wall. Each kid had his own nail with his name over it. The kids thought this was just peachy. We put a bucket under each crock but somehow that hallway floor got as muddy as any clam flat on the coast of Maine. Stan came to the rescue and bored 3 or 4 holes in the floor to drain the water in the hall down to that cellar that looked like "Tobacco Road.".

There is one advantage to an old rundown school like this; you can pound in a nail, bore holes in the floor or move anything --- no one will complain. Any changes we made in this school were an improvement. Ginnie and I were on a mission in that school and we would make it better than we found it, and the kids were right there to help.

# Laura's Marinated Beans...

Mix together:
1 or 2 cans of green string beans
1 or 2 cans yellow string beans
1 small can of tiny peas
1 small onion chopped fine
2 or 3 pieces of pimiento

In a separate pan mix and boil for 5 minutes:
¾ cup sugar
2/3 cup vinegar

Add:
¾ cup oil
1 tsp. salt and pepper to taste

Mix all ingredients together and let set for 3 – 4 hours or serve hot immediately.

Recipes similar to this were popular 25 years ago, but this one is a little different and is my favorite.

# A First Class Operation...

Yarnell School had no working equipment at all. Would a school with no running water, no inside toilets or no central heating have a <u>mimeograph or copier</u>? Not likely. We came up with some plastic rubbery jelly that we poured into a cookie sheet and let it harden. We used special ink for the master copy that would ditto any paper we pressed on it. The first few copies were good enough but after 8 or 9 you could hardly read it. Then we had to heat that jelly again on Mr. Miller's kitchen stove, let it harden, and put the master copy on it again which took hours. It was a nuisance. No fun. I could write things on the board for my kids to copy and hope for the best, but Ginnie's kids were too young for that except for a few geniuses she didn't have. So she had to use that gelatin compound all the time, and every night she had that jelly roll pan fighting for space beside the boiled potatoes and the gravy on the kitchen stove.

I guess right there is one reason why I preferred older children who could do a lot for themselves. It all evens out because Ginnie didn't like the sticky discipline problems presented by older children. It used up all the gumption of both of us to keep up with these classes.

I made a bulletin board that I put up in one corner of the room where the walls were a different color. (Maybe they ran out of paint or never came back to finish the job.) I used this board for pictures and articles I found in the newspapers or magazines. This was all new to these children who had few ideas about world events or national news. I spent time every day talking these things over with the class. We discussed the World Series, air travel, special people and even horse races. The background of these kids was very limited. Few of them had ever been 25 miles to State College and few of them had seen a newspaper at home.

Then I wrote a new "Thought for the Day" on the blackboard: a new one every week. We always talked over these gems and when a 6th grader girl told me she was making a scrapbook of all these sayings, I thought I had won <u>big</u>.

# Potato and Sour Cream Casserole...

Peel and slice 9 medium potatoes
Cook until tender
Drain
Arrange slices in a 2 ½ quart casserole

Mix:
½ cup grated cheddar cheese
½ cup fine dry bread crumbs
Sauté 1 onion in butter

Add onion to cheese mixture and spread on potatoes

Mix:
1 tsp. salt
3 eggs beaten
1 ½ cups sour cream

Then pour over the top of potatoes

Bake 25 minutes in 350 degree oven

# How I Danced Around All Day...

I soon found out fast enough that teaching lower grades and handling 3 grades in one room was a challenge, big time. I was ring master of a 3 ring circus. I had to be sure the other 2 grades were given assignments to work on while I was busy with just one. When I gave out papers to use in one class the other 2 grades had theirs done all ready and what did I want them to do <u>now?</u> I was pedaling as fast as I could to keep everyone going. It was never ending! I had to be sure that the boy who went out to the privy did not take the whole roll of toilet paper out with him and why was he taking so long, or that the fire in the stove was burning bright but not burning the sock draped over the top, or that Richard's tooth was not aching too much even if I could not do anything about it. Every time I thought I was getting somewhere with long division in one grade I could feel a dozen eyes peeled on me from the other kids to tell them what to do next. I wanted to say "Just color anything, any color, I don't care what; count the panes of glass in the windows, go get a drink, go out to the toilet, bring in some more kindling wood, look up something in the dictionary!" I was dancing all over that room all day. This was not the most shining hour in my life. I began to think I had made a huge mistake being a teacher. Having summers off was not worth all this aggravation! Then I began to think about these individual kids, each one with his own baggage. I thought about Billy in the 5th grade who had no mother and looked after his 2 younger brothers in school, Robert, who got our stoves going every day, or Millie who made those cookies with the blue frosting for me. They were all good kids who needed every break we could give them. Here they were trying to talk like a State of Mainer like me, or even trying to stay out of the creek to please me. There was not a spoiled child among them.

I tried to teach them to better themselves by learning all they could and especially to improve everything around them even, sanding their desks, washing the windows and keeping the privies clean.

Teaching that year in Yarnell I worked my head off helping these kids, but in the end I learned as much as they did.

# Conveniences...

We tried to appreciate all the conveniences that Yarnell School presented. This was true of that load of coal that we got. Hadn't they delivered that right on the front steps where it was handy to lug into the school? And whoever put that hand water pump beside the front steps? That was really convenient --- it was outdoors but right beside the steps. And now we found a new convenience: it was a neat path from the schoolhouse to the 2 weather beaten privies out back. That path headed the kids in the right direction when they were in a hurry --- and you can't beat that for convenience. There were no signs BOYS --- GIRLS on those privies but the kids seemed to know which was which. Those toilets were perched on the hill at the upper side of the school.

They were leaning over and out of balance and it took a lot for those kids to get used to. Some of them never achieved that balance which was the reason their efforts were all on one side of the toilet seat. Right off quick, Ginnie talked Neal into scrubbing those seats with cleaning ammonia and strong yellow soap. Neal did it reluctantly and told Ginnie to make those kids <u>sit</u> on the toilet seats rather than <u>roost</u> on them. And that was a meaningful learning experience right there. One day Ginnie and I discovered that some of the kids had used up every single roll of toilet paper we had, draping it all around each privy like giant Christmas presents and all over and up and down the hill behind, not thinking of the hardship it would cause everyone. They used up every single roll they could find except the rolls that Ginnie and I kept on our desks for runny noses.

It was tough to get supplies from the county office in Bellefonte. You know how some people get when they are dealing out supplies --- just as if everything came out of their own pockets. It took an act of God to pry them loose from that toilet paper. One clerk said "But you got the year's supply that you are entitled to, where did it all go?" (Right around the toilets, sister.) Anyway, she gave us a carton or two (grudgingly) and it was up to us to keep track of it. From then on we kept one roll of the you-know-what in each room and the kids had to tear off as much as they thought they needed whenever they went out to use the facility. Not too delicate an operation, but it worked. When Katie, a frail little 9 year old with glasses perched on her little nose, left to go out back she said to me very worriedly, "But teacher, we don't got no sh__ paper." No one raised an eyebrow because it was true. I tore her off a few squares of T.P. and wished her good luck.

# Orange Beets...

Heat together:
3 tbs. butter
¼ cup orange marmalade
1 tbs. orange juice
1 tsp. lemon juice

When heated add
2 cups sliced cooked beets

Simmer for a time until all beet slices are covered with juice.

These are wonderful!

# How We Changed
# the Image of our School...

Our classrooms were in bad shape just like everything else in this school. We noticed that the last time the walls had been painted nothing had been taken down. Some aspiring Michelangelo had painted all around the pictures, the maps and even all around the flag.

The wooden floors, grimy and caked with mud never looked clean. I found a big bucket of that pea green colored oil sawdust that janitors use on wooden floors to soak up dirt. Spreading that compound heavily on the floor we let the kids do their stuff. They stamped and trod around in the stuff for a week to lift all the mud of 3 generations of kids. It did the job. We thought it was a breakthrough on the efficiency of our janitorial duties.

The schoolbell had its own limitations. It was a hand bell with a clapper and handle separated from the bell. It was a game for us to find all three parts of that bell when I needed it to ring outside for the kids to come in, 2 or 3 times a day; morning, recess and noontime. ( Did you ever hear a teacher calling kids in by calling "Yoo Hoo?") They loved to hide the clapper; without that I couldn't use it to call them in. It didn't bother me much, especially when some little 4th grader thought he had pulled a fast one on the teacher.

Ginnie and I had great plans to fix up the pupils' desks. I brought a lot of sand paper to school and showed my kids how to smooth out the deep gouges and lines and cracks on the tops of their desks which made it difficult for them to pass in neat papers. I showed them how to use the coarse sandpaper to smooth it out. The kids thought it was a terrific project and when the tops were ready, I let the kids varnish them. I insisted they bring in an old shirt of their fathers to wear backward to keep their clothes clean. When those desks were finished, all the kids were wildly pleased with  them and hardly let anyone touch them. And some day they would remember how to clean up an old piece of furniture.

Ginnie had her grades 1, 2, & 3 bring along old shirts, too. She had bought all colors of paint and each little kid painted a chair. Ginnie did the tables. The kids were remarkable. After Ginnie showed them how to do it, they really did a great job and they loved how the room took on a new bright image. The kids had a marvelous time choosing their own colors and dipping into the paint and slapping it on their little chairs.

Little by little we were cleaning up this forgotten old school. We were showing them how to make the best of bad situations and how much cleanliness and color could make a difference, I think all of these lessons were as valuable as any geography class. Not only that, the kids were having a wonderful time!

# Impossible Quiche...

Combine:
½ lb. bacon, cooked and crumbled
1 cup Swiss cheese
1/3 cup chopped onion

Sprinkle the mixture evenly in a greased 9" pie pan

Blend:
2 cups milk
½ cup Bisquick
4 eggs beaten
¼ tsp. salt and a little pepper

Pour biscuit mixture into pie pan spreading over the bacon mixture

Bake until golden about 45-55 minutes

Let stand 5 minutes before cutting

Julie Tufts

# The Resident Mouse...

Every day after lunch, with the kids all seated at their desks, it was my time to read to the class. I loved this time when I could share wonderful stories --- sometimes the children's classics that I knew these kids would never be exposed to any other way. I read 15 books to them that year. Some were about animals, some about long-ago kids, some about far away places and some about children their own age. We discussed every story and some of the kids drew pictures of the action. They loved most everything about the books and I hoped it would encourage reading on their own. I made a little library in the back of the room, scrambling books from everywhere.

One day when it was very quiet except my voice reading the stories, a little mouse ventured out of the firewood stacked behind the STOVE. He ran all over the wood and disappeared into a hole in the floor. The next day I let the kids leave a few tiny crumbs on the wood, hoping the little mouse would come back. When I read, the mouse returned on the wood, found the crumbs and standing on his hind legs held that little crumb in his paws while he nibbled and chewed. Of course, the children liked it all. Turning it into a learning experience, I read them a poem about mice and then asked all of them to write their own poem about our visitor.

The next day (why didn't I see this coming?) a 5th grader gave me a note from his mother who said it was crazy giving crumbs to a mouse and then making up a poem about it. She said she wanted her child to be learning something in school all day instead of this foolishness about a mouse. I knew she would never understand that the children would be using their imaginations, learning new words, and enjoying the whole thing. At the beginning I did have a few worries that our mouse would bring along some of his relatives or in-laws to share, but it never happened. We saw only this one.

And this is the poem I read ---

*Little mouse in gray velvet*

*Have you had a cheese breakfast?*

*There are no crumbs on your coat.*

*Did you use a napkin?*

*I wonder what you had to eat.*

*And who dresses you in gray velvet.*

By Hilda Conkling

# Karen's Pineapple Au Gratin...

Combine:
2 large cans pineapple chunks
2 cups grated cheese

Put mixture into a shallow 9" x 13" pan that can be brought to the table.

Mix:
1 cup sugar
6 tbs. flour
Stir into pineapple mixture
Stir in 6 tbs. pineapple juice

<u>TOPPING</u>

Mix:
2 cups crushed Ritz crackers
2 sticks butter

Cover pineapple chunks with topping

Bake at 350 degrees for 20 minutes or until bubbly
Do not over bake

Serve warm

This is so good!

# Richard...

The people of this area in the Pennsylvania hills were mostly farm people with some working in the iron mill in the nearby town. This was 1950. As long as the kids ate well and slept well, parents didn't seem to worry much about dental care. I suppose they did the best they could.

Richard, a 5th grader had toothaches very often. I could always tell when the pain in his jaw was bad. Then he sat with one hand on his cheek, rubbing it now and then, and not participating in any classroom activity. I agonized with him and wished I could help him. Teachers are not allowed to give children any kind of medication but I figured the old remedy, ground up cloves, was acceptable. I gave Richard some of this and showed him how to pack it into his tooth. (Actually he had many bad teeth.)

That boy was so grateful; he claimed it helped a lot. Then I kept a bottle of cloves in my desk all the time for him. I couldn't understand why his parents hadn't done something about it until I learned he was one of 17 children.

# Incredible Mushroom Casserole...

1 lb. fresh mushrooms, cleaned and sliced in thirds
2 small diced onions (optional)
4 tbs. butter
1 tbs. flour
4 tbs. grated Parmesan cheese
1 egg
½ pint light cream
1/8 tsp. garlic powder
¼ tsp. celery salt
3 ounces cheddar cheese sliced
1 cup plain bread crumbs

Sauté mushrooms (onions) in butter just until juicy.

Remove from heat

Cool slightly

Sprinkle in flour and Parmesan to form paste mixture

Place in bottom of casserole dish

Mix egg, cream, seasonings in small bowl

Pour over mushroom mixture, cover with cheddar, then with bread crumbs

Bake covered for 20 – 30 minutes until bubbly.

# Lunchtime...

Lunchtime was a surprise every day for Ginnie and me. I don't mean our lunch because we had peanut butter sandwiches every day anyway because it saved us a lot of time when we didn't have to choose between tuna, bologna or egg salad. I mean it was a surprise to see what the kids brought for their lunches.

Most of them had cold cocoa in a wide mouth glass jar just wide enough to dunk their doughnuts and sandwiches. One boy brought in a hunk of cold fried liver and sometimes cold fried onions. They all got dunked the same way. Eventually the cocoa had pieces of greasy liver or a slice or two of fried onions, floating on top. Awful, and I'll tell you it didn't do a thing for my appetite when I realized that all the baked goods, cookies, cakes or biscuits had been made with chicken fat.

One day, 6th grader Millie brought me a special treat that she had made. It was a huge (big as a pancake) flat sugar cookie with royal blue frosting on top. One bite and I knew some unlucky hen had given its all for this cookie... Millie was so proud to bring me something that she had made herself. I stood there beside her and told her she had done well. I ate every last crumb and I told her I liked it a lot.

She beamed---

# Mitzi's Creamy Tomato Soup...

1 small diced onion
2 stalks diced celery
4-5 small diced carrots
2 - 3 garlic minced cloves
Olive oil and 2 tbs. butter
2 -3 pounds fresh tomatoes or 2 large cams Italian plum tomatoes
Salt and pepper
1 cup chicken stock
1 pint whipping cream

Sauté onion, celery and carrots in olive oil and butter until soft and slightly golden

Add tomatoes, chicken stock, salt and pepper to taste.

Bring to boil, turn down heat and allow to simmer. The longer it simmers, the more intense the flavor.

Puree mixture to desired consistency

Add cream and reseason to taste

Enrich further by adding 2-3 tbs. butter before serving

# Round, Round, Ready, Touch...

There was strange thinking in this area about school. We were supposed to get along with out-of-door privies, no inside plumbing, broken equipment, no window shades, desks with no bottom, doorknobs off, no playground toys and rags stuffed into the outside ventilators. <u>But</u> -- we had an expensive penmanship system that had to be followed. Once a month we let out school at noon so that we could attend a session of PENMANSHIP TRAINING given by the Martinsburg Writing System. Ginnie and I were happy enough. We had a half day off from school to spend in a real town with grocery stores and a post office. That was high living! We met all the other teachers in the district. Actually, everyone wanted to look us over. Word had gotten around that there were 2 young women from Maine teaching out there in Yarnell and they'd been hearing stuff.

The instruction was handled by a short stocky man (actually fair, fat and forty was more like it) who took this penmanship very seriously. After he gave us a pep talk he went into his song and dance about writing the Martinsbury Penmanship way. He stood up there in his wing tipped shoes and pinky ring with a blue fake sapphire stone in it, in the front of this room full of teachers and 2 new women from Maine. He held his arm and hand in the air, and with a piece of chalk, he circled in the air to the monotone of "Round, Round, Ready"--- and then on the word "Touch" 1-2-3-4" he made the 1-2-3-4 circles on the blackboard. We were expected to do the same with pencil and paper. I felt ridiculous with the whole drill but I did it. I just appreciated an afternoon off with a cup of coffee at the end. Also, we learned we had to submit every month a sample of penmanship from each pupil and we were to be evaluated by this little weasel who was running the show. It didn't make much sense to me that this Round, Round, Ready, touch 1-2-3-4 routine would do very much for these kids who were so far from any delicate routine like this. Maybe it was a good concept of using hands and fingers gracefully to form beautiful letters. I could do that --- and I did.

# Julie's Cheese and Bacon Frittata...

Beat together:
6 eggs
1 cup milk
1 green onion minced
½ tsp. salt

Pour mixture into a greased pan

Spread on top:
1 – 4 ounce pkg. shredded cheddar cheese
½ cup crispy bacon (cooked)

Bake at 400 degrees for 20 minutes

# And We Got a New Flag...

We had been teaching in that Yarnell School for a while when we thought it was time to get some swings for our school children. All they had to play with outside were the 2 big balls that we had bought for them. We thought that maybe if they had 3 or 4 swings to play on they wouldn't wander into that creek as much; or maybe they wouldn't spend so much time rooting in that pile of coal.

We looked around for some boards or posts for the swings but we couldn't come up with a thing. Then it dawned on us --- we could use the flag pole in the school yard. That pole was leaning over northeast, and what's more we didn't have a flag anyway. So --- come bright and early on a Monday morning, that flag pole was on its way down. After I stationed all the kids out of danger,

I let the 6th grade boys take turns sawing on that old flag pole that was destined for a new lease on life.

About the time the old flag pole was on its way down, a big West Penn Power Company truck drove by, slowed down, and backed up for a better view of the action. They thought it was a real sight; 60 kids on one side while boys were working on the pole with a dull saw. We, of course, didn't ask anyone's permission to do this; it didn't seem to us that anyone cared. Those Power Company men solved our problem in no time. They said they would come back soon and build 4 swings, ropes and all. What's more, they would put up a new flag pole. And they did. They made handsome swings with new rope and new hardware to make them slide smoothly.

Next came a new flag pole, and on that Saturday some war veterans brought us a new flag and dedicated it. We made the Centre County News. We had made it big time. The kids got new swings and all of us had the flag. The kids were so happy. In good weather every day the kids lined up around the pole while a chosen kid --- they took turns--- pulled up the flag, we saluted and sang America. Those kids were thrilled and I was proud of every one of them...

# Carrot Soup...

4 diced carrots
1 medium sliced onion
1 sliced stalk celery with leaves

Simmer all together in 1 ½ cups chicken broth
with cover on

Transfer to blender and add:
1 tsp. salt
½ cup cooked rice
Cover – turn blender on high

Slowly add ¾ cup light cream.

Serve garnished with snipped parsley

# How That Farmer
# Lost 5 Pounds of Bacon...

My classroom was on the side of the school building next to a thriving farm with just a rusted wire fence between us and a big herd of Holsteins. It looked picturesque and peaceful until the flies going from one contented cow to the other and to the school drove the kids crazy. Then I realized why the windows were nailed shut.

One day that fall we looked out the windows and saw 5 or 6 big hogs heaving clumsily down the road past the school in a steady trot, enjoying their freedom on a nice autumn day. I let the 6th grade boys --- 5 of them --- leave school to corral the black and white pigs. It seemed like a good thing to do at the time, you know, public relations and all that. It was quite a workout for both parties --- the pigs and the kids. Those pigs must have been exhausted with all these boys scrambling around after them, running around all afternoon. They ran around houses and through gardens and down the street with the boys not far behind. The kids had a wonderful time and it was the first Pig Race I had ever seen. All of us back at school took up places in the windows watching the whole operation. It was the wildest thing since Elvis joined the Army.

Since our school did not have Physical Education, I felt that exercise chasing pigs counted for a weeks' worth of organized sports. And what's more, every one of those pigs ran off 5 pounds of bacon that afternoon.

# Marilyn's Holly Delights…

Mix together and melt in a double boiler:
¼ pound butter or oleo
35 large marshmallows
1 tsp. vanilla
½ tsp. green food coloring

When it is cool, thoroughly mix in a bowl with 3 ½ cups of corn flakes.

Butter hands and shape into small wreaths and place on waxed paper.

Shape fairly quickly while the mixture is still warm.

Decorate with red candies

Another great one for kids --- under supervision of course!

# We Went to the Circus...

In the spring of our year in Pennsylvania we went to the circus in State College. It was a lovely warm day when we paid our admission and wandered down the main way, looking at all the sights and side shows that we might want to see. We stopped at one side show where a beautiful girl with bangles and sequins stood beside her partner with a dazzling display of swords and knives. It seemed like a good plan to pay our dollar and go inside the tent to see the big stunt. And this was the action.

The man (you know, the man with all the swords) showed the audience a tall size basket. He helped the spangled lady into it and fitted the top on the basket. So far so good. Then the man selected one sword after another and thrust each sword gingerly through the basket. The crowd clapped and whistled with enthusiasm. This was a clever trick, we could see that. Just when all was going smoothly the man was shoving the last and biggest sword into that basket; we all were surprised to hear the sequined queen in the basket scream and scream. Everyone laughed and clapped sure it was part of the act. Not me. When that girl climbed out of the basket we could see blood running heavily down her neck. That hot tent and the sight of all that blood were too much for me and I left the tent and went outside where I passed out cold. There I was on the runway of the girlie show with Stan pouring Coca Cola (that he had grabbed from a by-stander) down my face and my 5 year old daughter screaming at the top of her lungs. It was not the most fun I ever had.

The next day the <u>Centre County News</u> carried the news of the accident at the circus and how the sequined queen was recovering at the hospital. No one mentioned the woman who passed out and I was glad of that.

Going to the circus in May was at the end of our year in Yarnell. It had been a hard year at school, but I was always happy to remember the children.

# Lancaster, New Hampshire 1959-1968

# Six

## Stan and Me...

Stan and I were high school sweethearts and best friends, too. During the war he was a lieutenant in the Navy, serving on a destroyer escort that, with other ships convoyed large cargo ships to Africa and the Mediterranean. They made 10 trips which were pretty routine but not without danger from German U-Boats and fighter planes. They were thankful when DE 258 did not take a direct hit.

In 1944 between these trips to the Med Stan and I got married. After the war Stan earned 2 more degrees and became a school administrator in New Hampshire. As his career progressed we lived in Pembroke, Lancaster and Charlestown New Hampshire. Schools and education had a big place in our home. There were many tales to tell.

# Which Twin Had the Toni?...

My husband Stan had his share of extraordinary teen age behavior at the school in Lancaster where he was principal. One year there were 2 sisters, twins in the freshman class. Each one of the girls had a thick long braid that reached to her waist. Those braids were as thick as the girls' wrists. One day that class was putting together a play and the kids were standing around back stage when the worst possible scenario took place. One boy dared another kid to cut off the braid of hair on one of the twins. That braid was gorgeous and had probably taken at least 10 years to grow; each girl was tall and those braids were long. It seemed like a fun idea and all the kids gathered around to watch the dare take place. It took a while to get that hair hacked off with a jack knife while the other twin ran to the office and called her father who was a technician at the hospital. The first that Stan knew about the calamity was when the father whipped into the school yard in his Cadillac, and jumped out of his car leaving the door swinging wide open. He raced into the office and yelled "Who is the GD – kid who cut off my daughter's hair?" at the top of his lungs. (Tells your right there this was a problem.) So Stan and the distressed father looked around the place. By this time the kids had scattered and the culprit, who was desperate, had beat it and gone to the Rectory of the Catholic Church up the street and told the priest what a mess he was in. There wasn't much he could do about the hair. It was "Good night Irene" to that braid

That evening the boy's father, who happened to be the Chief of Police in town, called our house to apologize for his son's actions. His final words were "I know there has to be a horse's a__ in every crowd but why is it always that boy of mine?"

One happy ending to this was when the other twin had her braid cut off by her mother. Apparently the girls thought it was a wonderful idea.

For a few days Stan heard from school board members who said they didn't know he had put in a new course in barbering in the high school.

# Graduation Punch...

During those years when Stan was principal of the schools in Lancaster, New Hampshire, we had a "graduation tea" at our house every year after the Baccalaureate Service on the Sunday before graduation. We invited the graduates, the school committee and the high school faculty, making a total of about 65 -70 guests. This is the punch recipe that I made up for those annual affairs.

For 5 gallons of punch.......

8 small cans frozen lemonade plus water called for on the can.....makes 8 quarts

3 bottles concentrated Zarex (any flavor) mixed with 13 pints water and 4 quarts ginger ale

Makes 20 quarts or 5 gallons. I figured 5 gallons made about 125 small punch cups. You can add cherries or strawberries for color.

# Cranberry Punch...

In a punch bowl, combine:
2 pints softened sherbet
Juice of ½ of a lemon
2 cups orange juice
¾ cup of sugar

Stir to dissolve sugar

Add 1 ½ quarts cranberry juice (48 ounces)

Before serving punch add 2 – 28 ounce bottles of ginger ale or champagne

Mix well

Scoop remaining sherbet into balls and float on top of the punch

Makes 30 – 4 ounce servings

# Charlestown Junior High School…
# 1970 – 1977

# Seven

# What Car Did You Buy?...

In 1970, when I started teaching at Charlestown Junior High in New Hampshire, I was the "new kid on the block" for the teaching staff. I was given 5 classes; two of which were lower groups or "academically challenged" as the administration liked to call it.

One of my classes was an 8th grade math group; 10 boys 13 to 15 years old. I could not believe it when I read over the textbook "Number Theory." for that class. They couldn't mean that book for these kids. It would be as ridiculous as trying to teach Eskimos how to make french fries. I knew I had to make up a different program to fit these boys. I hunted up some old math books in storage under the stairs. True --- these books had old pictures and illustrations of 1950s people, woman in pearls and high heels making pies and using fractions and men in coat and tie measuring for new linoleum. These books were basic lessons about fractions, long division and 3 cases of percentages; never mind number theory. I couldn't imagine how number theory would help these boys figure out a cord of wood or how many shingles it would take for a new garage. Then they might need to know sooner than later.

One day the guidance counselor in the school saw me using the old books and went into a tailspin telling me how out of date these books were and it wasn't fair to my class not to have new books. He was a gold mine of useless information. He was sure he could run the British Isles if he had a chance. As far as I could see the only thing he had going for him was clean fingernails. He rattled on with a full head of steam, asking me if the principal knew about this. I told him the principal helped me find the books and they were working very well.

For a while this class reviewed and drilled the multiplication tables and the addition facts. It was time for me to swing into action. I had to come up with a plan that I could sell to this crowd of boys, but it was no trip to Niagara Falls I can tell you that.

First I brought to class a stack of daily newspapers, one for each boy who had never really glanced at a newspaper before this. To these boys, the newspapers were rare. We looked over every section; the sports, the obituaries and the classified ads. Then they went into overdrive when we took in the automobile sales sections. For them that was as good as a bologna sandwich with lots of mustard; it was their turf. I told the boys to study over these ads and then decide which advertised car he would like to buy. It was no surprise to me when most of them wanted to buy a pickup truck. I asked them to share with the class what choice they had made and why they wanted that particular pick up truck. Was it the price or the model?

We talked about selling prices and rate of interest on their car loans. They figured out what car payments would be and how much they had to pay for the taxes, registration and car insurance. Those boys would be doing these things themselves in a year or two. They loved all of this! They talked about these cars as if they were real; what mileage they were getting and how much it would cost to fill up with gasoline. Soon they asked how much it could cost to build a garage for their cars. So we figured that out, too.

Other stuff we talked about was withholding tax, health insurance and checking accounts. This was a whole new world for this class. I turned them loose with LL Bean catalogs and they made out orders for clothing they might like; imaginary orders for hunting jackets and boots. We talked about everything in this class. There never was a discipline problem here because the kids really enjoyed these projects. Since some of them had had a hard time in life, I wanted them to know all these facts of life. But not sex. They told me they had watched the flies in the sugar bowl for that.

During Halloween week I discouraged them from slashing tires. I told them it was a cop-out; it didn't take any brains to ruin somebody's tires and did they want the tires on their "new" cars slashed? Why couldn't they figure out some fun that wasn't destructive? They ended up throwing rotten tomatoes at the hogs at the pig farm. They said the tomatoes made a big splat when they connected with the pigs' backsides. I felt sorry for the pigs but we had made some progress; most anything was better than slashing tires.

In all our talks about cars and money and life, they knew I was on their side all the way. One day David, a big 15 year old, edged up to my desk and said, "I really like that blue dress you wear with the big red flowers on it." This from a kid who had wanted to slash tires. These boys had come a long way.

# Lasagna...

Brown 1 lb Italian sweet sausage

Spoon off fat then add:
1 clove garlic minced
1 tbs. whole basil
1 ½ tsp. salt
2 cups canned tomatoes
2 – 6 ounces cans tomato paste

Simmer all for 30 minutes.

Cook 10 ounces lasagna noodles until tender: drain

Combine:
3 cups Ricotta cheese
½ cup grated Romano cheese
2 tsp. parsley flakes
2 beaten eggs
2 tsp. salt
½ tsp. pepper

Place half the noodles in 13" x 9" x 3" baking dish

Spread with half the cheese filling

Add ½ lb. mozzarella cheese and half the meat sauce

Repeat layers, ending with mozzarella cheese.

Bake at 375 degree about 30 minutes.

Let stand for 10 minutes before serving.

My favorite recipe for family get-togethers
Makes a lot

This is the only lasagna recipe I use. It takes a lot of time but it is worth it and makes a lot for a crowd.

# How I Got Rid of that Motorboat...

In this school I taught Social Studies to classes of sixth graders. The kids in this class were pretty average which was lucky for me because there was one amazing personality to deal with. There was <u>Jimmy</u> whose claim to fame was taking on a different personality every day. I kid you not. One day of the week he would be an <u>ape</u> and swing into my room, bent over with his arms pounding on his chest, doing what he thought was an ape's mating call. At least that is what he was trying to do. How did I know? I never had heard an ape's mating call in my life. Other days he might be a race car (vroom, vroom) or a zooming motor cycle at full throttle, a Harley at least.

I can tell you, it gave me the creeps. He did this so often he had these ungodly personalities down pat. Some days, one of the girls in his class would get to my desk first --- ahead of Jimmy and announce to me his personality of the day.

One morning, Katie reported to me that Jimmy was a motorboat that day. Then, sure enough I could hear him coming down the hall. "Putt --- Putt --- Putt." Usually he would quiet down after he had been in class for a while but not today. The putt --- putt ---putt of that motor boat went on too long and I dreaded the day when he would be a Sherman tank. My patience had run out. It's hard to teach a lesson about Alaska or any other place in the world amid that monotone putt---putt---putt. I was ready to blow! If I couldn't quiet him down I could put him away from me. So I moved his desk and chair and Jimmy himself out in the hallway for the rest of the class period. I gave him a book to cover the law (not depriving him of an education.) He may have taken that motorboat out with him, but with my door closed I couldn't hear it.

When school was over for that day and I was dragging his desk and chair back into my room, I noticed something written on the wall. Above that desk in large magic marker letters was "I hate old Fatso in this room" with an arrow pointed to my room. There was no doubt who Fatso was! ME!, and I wasn't crazy about him either. We were on a collision course and there was no one around handing me a double dose of Tylenol. I knew I had to figure out a way on my own to manage Jimmy and all those characters he was bringing to class. Then I remembered he had told the class about the "tumbler" he got for Christmas, you know the machine that tosses and tumbles rocks around in a jar and makes them smooth. I took a great interest in that machine and asked him all about it. I took to school some rough turquoise stones I had brought from Arizona and asked if he would like to work on those. I could see his eyes light up when I gave the stones to him for his own. Now and then he would bring to class a piece of the turquoise he had smoothed and I had him explain to the class how he did it.

Instantly our relationship got better. From then on Jimmy tried to please me. He never again brought that motor boat to class. That worked for me.

# Stuffed Pork Chops...

Sauté 4 pork chops in a large frying pan

When pork chops are almost done, place in shallow baking dish, leaving the pork chops' drippings in the fry pan.

Mix 1 can mushroom soup with drippings, adding a little water.

Mix 1 pkg. chicken stuffing mix according to directions on the pkg.

Place 1 ½ tbs. stuffing on each pork chop

Ladle pork and soup mixture over the top of stuffing.

Place baking dish in 350 degree oven for 25 – 30 minutes.

# This is GOD...

The science room was located at the back of the school building with school grounds all around it. There was a half grown tree --- a maple tree out there that was just great for climbing. It was an attractive nuisance for the kids who loved to climb. It was a problem to keep them out of that tree and kids were bawled out for it all the time.

One day Bill, the science teacher, looked out the window of his empty classroom at lunch time and saw a 5th grader having a great time trying to reach the top of that tree. That 5th grader was a chubby kid, huffing and breaking off branches. Actually he was fat and was having a hard time of it. Quietly Bill opened the window close by the tree, hid behind the window and yelled in a deep threatening gruff voice "Kid! This is GOD --- get out of my tree!" Terrified, that boy scrambled himself down as fast as lightening in a thunder shower, clipping and smoothing out tree branches on the way down with the seat of his pants. When he made it to the ground he furtively looked around and beat it to the other end of the building. All the kids who were watching the climber heard GOD too. They scuttled themselves far and wide out of there.

Bill had no more trouble keeping kids out of that tree. Word got around.

# Haddock in Shrimp Sauce...

Place 1 lb. haddock in a 13" x 9" cooking pan or casserole

Pour 1 can of shrimp soup plus ¼ cup milk over the haddock

Bake at 350 degrees for 25 – 30 minutes

This makes an attractive and flavorful way to cook haddock.

Use a casserole dish that can be brought to the table.

# A Red Derby Hat...

One day our music department hosted a concert given by a Boston school. These Massachusetts city kids sang and played in their band very well. Too bad they swaggered and bragged all day --- in the halls and in the cafeteria. They obviously were putting down our country kids. I noticed one of the older boys from the city wore a jazzy red satin derby hat all day. He was hard to miss! Our New Hampshire kids were subdued and in awe, feeling like poor country cousins (with hang-dog looks on the faces.) They were as droopy as tired tossed salads with sagging shoulders on most of them.

After the visiting musicians left, I got my homeroom kids together and closed my class room door with a planned flourish. They knew when I did that, there was going to be big stuff.

It was part of my act to get their attention. Then I asked:

How many of you have a pond or swimming pool at your house or nearby?

How many of you have a snowmobile?

How many of you can ride a horse?

How many of you can ride bikes all over town?

And then they realized what I was getting at. Those city kids weren't so big after all and anyone could buy a red satin derby hat.

# Apricot Chicken...

Remove skin from 3 whole chicken breasts which have been halved

Arrange in 13" x 9" baking dish

Sprinkle with salt and pepper

Blend together:
1 - 21 ounce can of apricot pie filling
1 tbs. lemon juice
½ tsp. salt
½ tsp. nutmeg
½ cup pecan halves

Pour mixture over the chicken, cover and bake at 375 degrees for 50 – 60 minutes

Arrange chicken on rice

Spoon mixture on top

# Carl...

Carl Perkins was a 7$^{th}$ grader, a blonde good looking farm kid. Not crazy about school but he did what he was told to do and was good natured about it. As solid as <u>State Farm Insurance</u>, he never got into trouble and was happy in his back row corner seat. It was "his" corner.

One day after lunch before class started, I saw Jim Sawyer, another 7$^{th}$ grader, tricky and cool as a cucumber, strolling importantly around the room for no apparent reason. I thought he was cruising along looking for trouble and I watched him. When he got to Carl's desk he knocked Carl's books and belongings all over the floor. Carl jumped up like he was shot; grabbed Jim by his shirt and said, "Listen, Sawyer, the next time you come dancing up by my desk knocking my stuff on the floor, I'll throw you down on your ass!"

In my mind I congratulated Carl. I pretended I hadn't heard a thing. Carl settled his own problem. Sometimes, it is better that way.

# Zesty Sausage...

Spray a sauce pan with cooking spray,

Combine 1 jar (12 ounce) apricot preserves and 2/3 cup spicy brown mustard and cook over low heat, stirring for 5 minutes.

Add 1lb. fully cooked smoked sausage links --- cut diagonally in bite size pieces

Simmer for 15 minutes, stirring now and then

Serve hot either in a casserole dish or a chafing dish with picks.

# Soap and Water...

One year at that school, I had a reading class of 9 sixth grade girls, a little on the slow side. Most of them came from below average homes. These girls needed a lot of practical attention in most every way and I wanted to give them extra help.

That group came to my classroom following noon recess every day. They had played hard outside and very often they were hot and sticky and smelly. Wow! I needed to do something besides teaching reading to that group. They liked to discuss all kinds of things and we could do that in that group of girls only, I figured now was a good time to talk about personal health, where else could they learn these things? Not in a mixed class of boys and girls. And not in

Physical Education because all they did there was play basketball, never using the showers. (I knew that because the girls' locker room was right next door to my room.) So we talked a lot about how they were growing up and how they should pay attention to baths or showers. They all agreed and these 12, 13 and 14 year olds seemed to be convinced about soap and water. I thought that lesson was a job well done.

Well, forget that. The next day the principal looked me up to tell me he had had a phone call from a mad mother who said it was none of my business whether these kids took more baths or even talked about soap and water. I was supposed to teach reading and would I let alone health subjects? So that was that when I learned that her daughter Anna didn't have much of a chance to take a shower at home anyway. It seems that the parents and kids lived in 2 trailers put together to accommodate his children, her children and their children.

Soon after all that, Anna came to me very quietly one day, and said "Do you think I could use the shower in the girls' locker room?" Yay! I had a breakthrough! I told her I would speak to the other teachers for their permission for her to leave study hall. I told her I would keep a paper bag with towel and soap in my desk drawer just for her. She could come to my room very quietly any time and take out of my desk drawer the paper bag with a towel and her own Lifebuoy soap. She was so happy about it. After that, lots of times, I could see her taking the bag out of my desk drawer, and returning with a shiny face and hair soaking wet. It was one of the best lessons I ever taught. I won and Anna won too.

# Roberta's $1000 Prize Casserole

## Devil Chip Casserole...

1 large pkg. medium macaroni shells
1 large can of deviled ham
16 ounce sour cream
1 egg
2 tbs. minced onion
½ stick butter
½ # bacon, well cooked and drained until crisp
1 cup finely crushed potato chips
1 ½ cup sharp cheddar cheese well chopped

Cook macaroni shells. Drain water off and leave in sauce pan

Add butter and toss until macaroni is lightly coated

Set aside

In a small bowl combine:
Sour cream
Deviled ham
1 egg

Beat together until blended

Place half of macaroni in a well greased casserole

Cover with half of deviled ham mixture

Toss lightly with half of the cheddar cheese, sprinkle with half of the potato chip crumbs which have been thoroughly mixed with the crumbled bacon and minced onion

Repeat layers ending with the potato chip mixture

Bake 25 minutes covered and 10 minutes uncovered in 350 degree oven

Serves 6

When my friend Roberta, a professional cook, was a stay-at-home Mom, she entered all kinds of cooking contests. After she had sent in many recipes that didn't win, she sent in this one, "Devil Chip Casserole", signed her husband's name, and he won a chance in the "Bake Off." Roberta coached him well and he won the grand price $1000, for her recipe!

# My Lunch Is Better Than Yours...

The teachers in that school were a friendly bunch, professional in their work and mostly in good humor. The Staff Room was across the hall from my classroom in the basement, so I heard it all. Most of the teachers spent time there every day. The room had 2 or 3 lounge chairs and a heavy long table where we ate our lunches or solved a few problems. We had beginning teachers who were just starting their careers as well as the most of us who had been at it for a while. The discussions were lively and the arguments were loud, but it was all good natured keeping up with smart people. It was a fascinating place to be. I used to say it was the best show in town since Harry Truman wore Hawaiian shirts in Key West............................ One winter when things seemed to be slowing down, two of our young men teachers got into a big discussion of who had the best lunch from home. It took off, and things got really interesting. The next day Bill Johnson brought in a chicken salad in a crystal bowl with a white linen napkin covering it. The day following, John Tucker brought a full size linen table cloth and spread it out with a bone china cup and saucer for his coffee. (We had been using stained mugs.) After that, Bill brought a silver candelabra and a fancy plant for a centerpiece. Every day it got better and better until spring vacation time came around and Bill and Jim called it a tie.

Bill still kept his motorcycle in the teachers' room.

# Ann's Chicken Elegant...

Bring to a boil and simmer for 20 – 20 minutes:
3 large chicken breasts
1 to 2 cups of water
Celery tops, chopped onion, salt, bay leaf, and a little rosemary

When done, save cooking liquid. Remove bones and skin from chicken

Cut chicken into bite size pieces

Mix lightly with:
1 pt. sour cream
1 cans condensed cream of mushroom soup
1 small drained can of mushroom pieces
A few cut up pieces of pimiento

Spoon into a large casserole

TOPPING

Melt 4 tbs. butter in one cup reserved chicken broth

Stir in 1 8 ounce pkg. of seasoned stuffing mix

Spoon evenly over chicken in casserole

Bake at 350 degrees for 45 minutes

Casserole may be frozen before baking

# Vapo-Rub Fred...

In every school there are always kids who are normal mischief-makers in a small way. These are the ones who do funny stuff to make the other kids laugh or maybe just to stir up a little excitement. We will always have those, thank God. They are good kids all the way.

Then we have mean spirited kids who have their own problems big time with behavior that is off the wall. One of the worst in this school (or in any school --- he was that bad) was a new boy in Grade 8. He was shifty and full of anger. His name was Fred and he created havoc wherever he went. I don't think he did any school work because he spent most of his time in the principal's office or with the guidance director. A good indication that he had been in trouble before was the weekly visit of his own social worker, Mrs. Collins. One day when she came to see Fred, she brought him some new glasses. Fred took the glasses off, put them on the floor and jumped on them, smashing them to bits. He picked up the frames and coolly handed them to her. I couldn't imagine how patient she was.

Another day when Fred was sent to the office, Mr. Wilson, the principal tried yet another angle to approach Fred. Mr. Wilson tried being kind and understanding. Then Fred brought out of this pocket, a jar of Vapo-Rub (you know the stuff in the blue jar), rubbed it in his own eyes to show that he was tough and didn't care in spite of the burning Vapo-Rub.

Fred was sullen and sneaky. He did not have any friends that I knew of. The kids kept their distance from him. A severely troubled kid, Fred moved on to another school with another social worker. He left battle fatigue every where he went. I wonder how Fred is today.

# Pistachio Delight…

Mix together:
1 ½ cups flour
¾ cup walnuts
¾ cup butter or oleo

Pat into a 13" x 9" pan

Bake at 350 degrees for 20 minutes

Cool

Whip together:
1 - 8 ounce  pkg. softened cream cheese
1 cup powdered sugar
1 cup cool whip

Pour over cooled crust

Beat together:
2 pkg. pistachio pudding mix
2 cups milk

Pour over cream cheese layer

Combine rest of cool whip with ½ nuts

Spread on top and chill thoroughly.

# So --- Where Is Alaska?...

As a social studies teacher I was part of a panel to approve a new social studies book series for the 7th grade through high school. There were 4 young men teachers and I on the panel. I had looked through the entire new program and I didn't like what I saw. It seemed to me that the program was more psychology and sociology than facts. How could kids --- any age --- make valid conclusions about anything if they didn't have the background of knowledge to begin with? I held out for teaching basic geography and history. How would kids know where cities are? Or the Nile River? Or the Panama Canal? Or kangaroos in Australia? My colleagues came on like gangbusters for the new books and I was outvoted. They thought I was behind the times and told me that this was the new concept of social studies. This new program would teach the students where to <u>find</u> the facts. Can't you see kids graduating from high school with Britannica Encyclopedia draped around their necks when the information should be in their heads?

Well --- since I was outvoted, this expensive new stuff was passed around. I decided to go along with this and work with it the way I was supposed to. No maps, no wonderful stories of Lewis and Clark to the West (who were Lewis and Clark?) whaling out of Nantucket (where's Nantucket?) the Civil War (who won?)

The 8th graders got the new books and I put on a happy face and we read over the first chapter. OK, we did that, and then I read ahead to the suggested homework that was given. It instructed the kids to go through their neighbor's garbage or trash to learn what the neighbors were really like. What message would come up when used tea bags were found? Or empty mushroom soup cans? Or a bunch of empty soap wrappers? I would be barbecued if I sent the kids home with an assignment like this! It was like dump picking. This was too much for me. I had my class keep these new books in their desks to cover my tracks, but mostly we used the old books. Maybe that was old stuff, but it worked for me.

# Marilyn's Fried Dough...

Mix together:
3 cups flour
2 tsp. baking soda
1 tsp. salt

Then mix in:
6 tbs. shortening (Butter flavored Crisco is best)

Slowly add 1 cup warm water

Knead and mix well

Form in oval balls

Roll out and cut in squares

Deep fry and drain.

Serve with sugar and cinnamon.

## Bruce...

And along came Bruce, an 8th grade boy who came to my class sullen and difficult every day. He had the corner seat away from everyone. When he arrived at my room he would knock every seat on his way,. Helter skelter. Then he sat down with a pouting look on his face. I did a lot of writing on the blackboard and I expected the class to take notes. Bruce just sat there not moving. I asked him why he wasn't writing down a few things and he said he didn't have a pencil, I said, "Why didn't you tell me?" And he answered "Because you didn't ask me." You get the picture. A conversation like that can kill a good lesson. He was not my favorite kid; a shining light he was not. He was as irritating as a hang nail. You can always tell the kid who is looking for trouble. That kid made me so mad that my eyes would twitch.

About 6 or 8 years after, I was asking about some of my former students and I heard that Bruce had graduated from UNH (!!!) A former teacher told me that Bruce had asked him, "I wonder where Mrs. Tufts is now --- she was my favorite teacher."

A miracle --- you never know.

## Double Trouble…

There were twins, John and James in my 5$^{th}$ grade social studies class. They were both hyperactive; it seemed like they were strung on piano wire. They were not afraid of anything or anybody. When those two came through the door every day I pulled myself together for the aggravation I knew they would be. I thought someone hated me to go through this every day. Skinny little guys with tricky faces, they were always waiting to start something, jumping around like hoppy toads, irritating other kids, setting up confusion in the classroom. They came to my room just before lunch every day, which was significant because their morning pills to calm them down had worn off by then and they would get the next pill at noontime. By the time they came to my class just before lunch, they were winging it.

James would get a mouthful of water in the boys' locker room down the hall and hold it in his mouth until he let it go on the neck of another kid; starting a battle right there. Or John would sit there at his desk calm and peaceful as he was pulling hairs one at a time from the neck of the kid in front of him I was getting madder by the minute. I just wanted to shake those boys until their teeth rattled. In 1974 that was a no-no. Can't say that was progress. I was sure those two boys were headed for the rock pile. I changed their seats often so the same kids did not have to sit in front of them all the time. I'll tell you those boys were hard to love. All the psychology that I ever had did not prepare me for this and I felt I should get combat pay.

During that year at a retirement party for one of the older teachers, the guest of honor spoke a few words; and then she said in her next life she wanted to come back as a children's disease. I knew just what she meant. She probably meant those twins.

# Danny's 100 Meatballs (For 30 – 40 people)...

3 lbs. ground beef
1 ½ cups butter cracker crumbs
2 tbs. chopped parsley
Salt and pepper
3 large beaten eggs
½ cup minced onions
1 cup scalded milk

Mix together well

Form into firm bite-size balls

Bake in jelly roll pan at 350 degrees for 15 minutes

Serve with this sauce.

Heat together in a large saucepan:
1 cup ketchup
¼ tsp. pepper¼ cup cider vinegar
1 tbs. chopped onion
2 tbs. brown sugar
1 tsp. dry mustard
2 tbs. Worcestershire sauce
Few drops hot sauce to taste
½ cup water

Add meatballs, heat gently, and serve from a chafing dish

# Charlie and Thomas...

One year, in the 8th grade I had Charles Fritz and Thomas Romanski. Since they were best friends I seated Charles in one corner seat and Thomas in the other corner so they could get their work done. Once in a while they would have a falling out and were pretty mad at each other. Sometimes when that happened Charlie would stand up at this seat and yell "You Pollock!" and Thomas would stand up at his seat and answer "You Kraut, what do you know?" And silently they called each other "Kraut" and "Pollock" under their breaths all day long. The next day they were buddies again and sharing their lunch in the cafeteria.

# Candy's Whole Cooked Cauliflower…

Take leaves off a large head of cauliflower

Make a deep cut across the bottom ½" deep in an X shape

Place on a rack in bottom of heavy 4 qt. sauce pan

Put in about 1" of salted water

Steam for 15 – 25 minutes

Test with fork for doneness

To serve, place whole cauliflower on a serving plate

Pour cheese sauce down over the cauliflower

This is a good way to serve this vegetable
And it looks lovely too.

# The Way West...

Sometimes a very special production can be made of Social Studies lessons and it was that way in my 7th grade class. We were studying about the <u>Way West</u> when sturdy and courageous pioneers hit the Oregon Trail in wagon trains to settle new lands in the west.

The entire class would make up one wagon train, for which they would chose a wagon master as well as the scout. Then all the other kids would be members of families with their own covered wagons. They made maps of their travel and used these to check their progress as they met the hazards along the way. Often I would suggest problems that they would face. They met together around the campfire (don't worry --- we made believe my teacher's desk was their fire)   what would they do if someone got a snake bite? What would they do if the scout got lost and wasn't seen for 3 days? How would they cross that river? What if they knew that Indians were following their train? These kids in my class would never have those problems, but they might learn how to reason or solve other ones.

We figured out what each family would bring; the tools, the seeds, sometimes a favorite rose bush from their farms back east, and of course, their food.

Toward the end of our trail, we took over the Home Ec. lab and made up an evening meal for these travelers. We had beans, carrots, onions and potatoes. By then the pioneers would have used up their eggs so they didn't have cake. (They figured out perhaps they might have molasses cookies.) I brought in the antelope meat that the scout had shot. Actually it was stew beef that I bought at Ted's Market.

This is one of the best projects I ever had. The kids learned so much about map work, problem solving, the land west of the Mississippi and most of all --- working together. I hope there is a 45 year old person out there somewhere who can remember going west to Oregon in our 7th grade in 1975.

# Priscilla's Rich Biscuits...

Combine:
2 cups flour
3 tsp. baking powder
6 tbs. butter (real butter)

Add no more than 2/3 cup cream (half and half or light cream)

Bake at 400 degrees

These are <u>choice.</u>

These are a super lunch dish with stewed fruit and a cup of tea.

# We Landed in Hawaii...

In the 6th grade when the class was studying about Hawaii, I needed to think of a marvelous idea that would make Hawaii more real to these country kids in New Hampshire. We couldn't learn hula dancing --- half of the class were boys. We couldn't have a luau; where would we get the barbecued pig? Then I had a brainstorm! Why not let the kids make leis? You know, like they were arriving in Honolulu. Styrofoam white packing peanuts would be just the thing! They would be easy to find, everything came packed in that stuff. So I got hundreds of them from the science lab. (they had just received new equipment that was packed in it.) So we were off! I gave each kid 2 big handfuls of Styrofoam peanuts, passed around darning needles and Aunt Lyddy's thread, and the class went to work. Some of the kids colored the peanuts pink to make them more real. What a sight! 25 kids with those gorgeous hand made plastic leis around their necks! The kids loved it!

Well, that was before lunch; before those fell apart, before the leis collapsed. Those peanuts went flying all over the hallways, the cafeteria, the library, the gym, and even the office (which made the principal question the whole idea.) The entire student body got carried away with this bedlam. It was pretty exciting. But one thing is clear, I'll bet those 6th graders never forgot this lesson about Hawaii.

But --- the custodians hated me.

# Mitzi's Crab Stew…

Sauté 2 lbs. crabmeat in ½ cup butter

Gently add:
3 cups half and half
1 cup whipping cream
Pepper
Old Bay seasoning to taste
½ freshly squeezed lemon

Let simmer for 15 minutes or less

Make sure it does not boil.

This is a treat!

# Marty...

Several times every year I reminded every class that there would be no swearing in my room. I would never swear at them and I wanted no swearing from them. It worked very well and I had no problem at all until Tom --- one of the best kids I ever hoped to see --- spun off a G_D something. All I had to do was look at him and he said : "Yeah, I know. I'm on my way." As I had promised, anyone swearing would go to the office to the "cooling off" bench where an offender cooled his heels until the principal dealt with him.

Sometime after that we got a new 8th grade student in Tom's class who hadn't been told about my swearing rule. Anyway, soon after he joined that class, something went wrong for him and he cussed loud and clear. I didn't have a chance to say a word because Tom said it for me, "You'd better not swear in here because she won't allow it!" That day I let Marty stay in class because he hadn't heard the rule.

Marty was a skinny kid and like a Bantam rooster; here, there and everywhere. He wore wire rim glasses that had been bent out of shape. They were on the end of his nose, and I wondered how he could see anything. He made friends easily and everyone liked him. He told me about his wonderful job on Saturdays. He hitched a ride to Claremont 10 miles away --- to work at cleaning the theater. I could well imagine how he hit that theater like a cyclone and left it as clean as a whistle.

Just before Christmas that year he stayed after class one day and told me he had a Christmas present for me. He wanted me to stay in my room for a while until he could bring the gift to me. Soon after, 2 8th grade boys came to my room toting a heavy packing box. After they set it on the floor, I opened it and out popped Marty himself who said, "I am giving you myself for Christmas, Mrs. Tufts!" And I almost cried. I was touched.

I have wondered what became of Marty. Somehow I think he may own a fleet of snowplows or maybe a plumbing business that can clean out pipes that have been plugged up for a long time. Whatever Marty chose to do would be well done with a good natured grin on his face.

# Gary --- Change His Seat...

When the incoming 6<sup>th</sup> grade class swarmed into my room for the class one day, Gary, a sharp little kid, made a bee line for my desk. "You've got to put Frank somewhere else today! He's been sitting beside me all day and has been farting and pushing all that stink right over to me and I am tired of it!" All the time waving his arms to show me what Frank had been doing. "I don't want him sitting beside me anymore" he added. I changed his seat.

Gary and Frank were really best friends. Sometime after that the word <u>religion</u> came up. I asked Frank what the word meant and he said "We don't believe any of that stuff at my house." Quick as a wink Gary spoke up, turned around and said, "Yes Frank, I know that, but I am praying for you all the time." They were really good friends.

# Aggression Cookies...

## Makes a lot...

Mix together:
3 cups brown sugar
3 cups butter
6 cups oatmeal

Add:
1 tbs. baking soda
3 cups flour

Put all this in a big bowl

Then smash, mash, knead and squeeze

Form into balls and place on ungreased cookie sheet. Mash each ball with the bottom of a glass.

Bake at 350 degrees for 10 – 12 minutes

These can be frost with almond flavor frosting.

This is a good recipe for lots of kids or a large group.

# And Then There Were These...

• In my last school there was an 8th grade girl who came to school one day in a flesh colored T shirt and flesh colored pants that were as tight as Oscar Meyer Sausage casings. Three feet away she looked naked. Our principal, a no nonsense guy had a little talk with her and she wore her coat all day --- buttoned up to her chin.

• We had an older reading teacher who was very tough. She had driven her husband's 18 wheeler semi. She said that was easier to handle than the school cafeteria at lunch time. No question she was tough, but she was always fair and excellent in her teaching. The kids all liked her, too.

• At the Academy when the new math teacher was obviously pregnant the first day of school, the headmaster asked her when her baby was due. "Today" she said. She gave birth the next day and came back to school the day after. She said she needed the money.

• When I asked my 6th graders what the word "throb' means, one boy wrote "It's when you get hurt and where you get hurt goes "Ba boop. Ba boop, Ba boop." A good answer I thought.

• Peace signs, happy faces, mood rings and earth shoes that looked like gun boats --- these were the 70's. And the eighth grade boys were crazy over Farrah Faucett.

• Two boys in grade 7 kept a chess game going all the time. One of them had a magnetic board and when they had 5 or 10 minutes to spare, out came the board for a move.

• When I was teaching at Pembroke Academy in 1958, I noted that one sophomore student in my class, Priscilla, had been absent for a week. I checked with our principal who told me Priscilla's mother had died the week before. On the next Sunday afternoon, I scouted out where she lived in Hookset. I brought her a pan of brownies and sat with her for a while. When I left, I hugged her very tight. In 1990, when my husband died, I received a sympathy card from Priscilla. It had been 40 years since I had seen her or heard anything about her, but Priscilla had remembered me.

. At the end of the last year of teaching I was happy and very pleased that the Junior High Yearbook was dedicated to me. Not only that, it was presented to me with a little speech by a 6th grade boy who would hardly speak to anyone if he didn't have to. Somehow he and I had hit it off after he came to my room one morning and quietly told me his father had gotten a new wheel chair the night before. I could see he wanted to share his story with someone and I had been there.

# Along the Way...

By now you realize how I used my theory <u>Education Is Learning How to Live.</u>

Along the way, when I was teaching "Fiddler on the Roof" my classes learned about different cultures and the philosophy of "If I Were a Rich Man." When my 8th grade boys "bought" their cars, they learned practical knowledge they would need very soon. Or when we cleaned up that little school in Pennsylvania they could see how to make things better. And when we read the "Diary of Ann Frank", they admired her courage.

I wanted my classes to know how their lives could be better through education, and along the way I wanted these kids to enjoy learning everything they could that would help them have a happy life.

And what about the kids who have passed through my classes? I remember so many of them and wonder about their lives. Where are they now? How did life treat them? Which ones went far? Which ones would remember me?

There are several PhD's, a minister, many teachers and nurses, mothers and fathers. Some of them stand out. One of them was an 8th grade boy in Charlestown who was part of my "buying cars" class. He is now working as boss for the town highway crew. It will be no surprise to hear how dedicated he is to his job or to helping people. I knew he'd be good at that. And the Coakley boys in Yarnell --- are they running their father's big farm? And that wonderful 8th grade boy in Livermore --- where is he? And, of course, there is Sonny, my 8th grader in North Berwick. He graduated college and was an instructor at the technical school in Portland for over 30 years. I will bet he did it always with a smile on his face. And Eleanor in Kennebunk who told me once she was practicing the piano with "big chords" so that her hands would look veiny like mine.

I would like to know about all of them. Since moving back to Maine in 1977, I have met up with my former students often, even at a funeral when a former 8th grader recognized me after 40 years and said, "You haven't changed at all, Mrs.

Tufts." I wanted to ask her if I had looked like 75 in those days at KHS. I must have changed <u>some.</u> But my inspiration is still the same --- education is learning how to live --- and I hope my classes have benefitted from all I tried to teach them.

It was a long ride from 1942 to 1977.

# About The Author...

Betty Kennedy Tufts is a true "State of Mainer," born in North Berwick in 1922. She spent there, as she readily claims, a wonderful and happy childhood with her parents, grandparents, and aunts and uncles. After North Berwick High School, she graduated from Gorham, Maine State Teachers College, now the University of Southern Maine, and she became a Junior High School teacher of social studies. She taught in Maine, Pennsylvania, Massachusetts and New Hampshire.

Betty married Stan, her high school beau, who held school administrator positions in New Hampshire. With a great interest in interior decoration, they built or remodeled eight houses along the way. They retired in Wells, Maine where Betty had her own antique shop for 20 years. She also set up and sold at antique shows in New England. They had three daughters, seven grandchildren and four great grandchildren.

A widow now, living in Wells, Maine she enjoys her family, her church, friends and mostly, the humorous side of all things.

Author's first book was "Tales of North Berwick".

Printed in the United States
212216BV00001B/1/P

9 781438 912493